PRIORY CHAMBERS

(LTD) EST 1856

Taylor

THE
BAKER'S
DAUGHTER

THE
BAKER'S
DAUGHTER

TIMELESS RECIPES FROM
FOUR GENERATIONS OF BAKERS

LOUISE JOHNCOX

WITH A FOREWORD BY
ALBERT ROUX

MACMILLAN

For my father, and my mother, with love and thanks.

First published 2014 by Macmillan
an imprint of Pan Macmillan, a division of Macmillan Publishers Limited
Pan Macmillan, 20 New Wharf Road, London N1 9RR
Basingstoke and Oxford
Associated companies throughout the world
www.panmacmillan.com

ISBN 978-1-4472-4705-0

Copyedited by Salima Hirani at Giraffe Books
Art direction, styling and page design by Simon Daley at Giraffe Books
Food and author photography by Ian Garlick
Food styling by Kathryn Hawkins

All personal photographs are the author's own, or provided by the author's family.
The photograph of the baker's grandchildren, number 8 on page 19, is courtesy
of Mandy Marodeen.

Printed and bound in China

Visit **www.panmacmillan.com** to read more about all our books and to buy
them. You will also find features, author interviews and news of any author events,
and you can sign up for e-newsletters so that you're always first to hear about
our new releases.

contents

Foreword *by Albert Roux*   7

Introduction   10

The Baker's Little Helpers   20
Favourite Bakes for Children

When Peter Met Frankie   42
Love on a Plate

Customers as Cakes   60
Classic Tea Shop Cakes

Sweet Delights   80
Iconic Cakes and Tarts

Smashing the Oven   98
Sweet Satisfying Rewards

Little Pieces of Heaven   110
Edible Gifts

Baking With My Father   128
Bread, Pastry and Savoury Specials

The Baker's Hands   146
Comfort Cakes

Poschiavo and Pastry Chefs   164
European Pastries

My Baking Journey   180
Notes On Ingredients   184
General Baking Tips   188

Index   190
Acknowledgements   192

foreword

When I was first introduced to Louise she told me about her baking memoir based on her family's tea shop in Weybridge, Surrey. I was interested about the pastry chef tradition in her family so I asked her to send me a chapter. I found the writing enchanting, full of evocative stories about her family's English tea shop, recipes and customs.

Louise recreates a gentler era in this delightfully nostalgic book. She tells us how her father opened *Peter's* in 1958 and ran the tea shop with his wife, Frankie, for over forty years. Peter, a traditional baker, made all the cakes, bread and savouries while Frankie welcomed customers as though they were family members.

Louise brings this endearing family story vividly to life through the sights, scents and sounds of the bakehouse and tea room. Every recipe comes with a tea shop tale; where there is a cake, there is a memory. Some are happy, some are sad, and all are a poignant reflection of her family life.

Louise has an extraordinary baking heritage to draw upon – her parents, grandparents and great-grandparents all ran tea shops and were master bakers and confectioners. She gives wonderful insight into the difficult lives of her pastry chef ancestors, who originated in Poschiavo, a Swiss–Italian village. In search of work, they first travelled to Marseille, France, where Louise's great-grandfather was born, and then to England where they opened a series of tea shops. I was fascinated by this tale of emigration and passion for handcrafted food and pastries, because food and family have always been central to my own life.

At the age of fourteen I worked as an apprentice pâtissier, travelling to England when I was eighteen to work in the kitchen at Nancy Astor's home, Cliveden. I opened *Le Gavroche* in 1967, which my son, Michel Jr, now owns and runs. I greatly appreciate the dedication and long hours that go into creating and running family food businesses. There is something special about handing recipes down to the next generation and baking together.

At the start of Louise's journey she tells us she went in search of the family recipes from the tea shop only to discover bits of card and notebooks containing lists of ingredients in huge quantities – but no methods. Only through the process of baking with her elderly father was she able to recreate the actual recipes. This baking experience, with all the tastes and smells, helped her to bring the tea shop memories to life. For Louise, cakes trigger emotions, heartfelt and original. I know from my own experience, when you grow up surrounded by food you store up a vast memory bank of taste memories.

The tea shop may have closed, but Louise continues the family tradition by baking her father's trusted recipes. She has updated many of the recipes and includes her father's baker's tips, making this a personal and practical collection, with period and modern photographs.

A storyteller and a baker's daughter, Louise conjures up a childhood remembered primarily through cakes. This book is an enchanting account of the author's childhood in a tea shop, complete with authentic recipes. It is an affectionate memoir that will both entertain with stories from a bygone world of tea and cakes and inspire people to bake.

ALBERT ROUX, OBE, KFO

Florentines

½ lb Margarine   Boil then add
½ lb Sugar   ½ cup of milk or cream
½ lb Flaked Almonds
¾ lb peel
¼ lb Chopped Cherries
        Allow to stand
        then drop out on a tray   260°

Puff Pastry

pinch flour
salt
5-6 ozs butter
Lemon juice abt 1 teasp.
Cold water.

Flour & salt & break fat into
large marbles. add lemon juice
mixed. Stir with knife (when
try not to break lumps.) turn on
board & roll keeping edges as
possible. fold into 3 press edges
Keep air in & turn by to min
roll in opposite way & fold again
put by for 10 mins   (so leaves in all)

leave all night. Put water
and add fruit & sugar
slowly to boil over slow heat
... and simmer until
... Then add lemon juice
... minutes. Test

introduction

My life has been shaped by cakes, the ones baked by my father in our family's tea shop, *Peter's*, in Weybridge. For over forty years Peter Johncox made cakes, big and small, of all shapes and sizes; birthday cakes, wedding cakes, cream cakes, fancy cakes, plain sponges. He baked bread most days and handcrafted homemade chocolates all year round. In April 2012, twelve years after the tea shop closed when Dad retired, he died in a hospice, just around the corner from the shop. This loss was shattering for my family. But I soon discovered that it wasn't just the family who missed my father. The local community also mourned the baker, who, over the years had turned a simple tea shop into a welcoming home from home for all those who walked through the doors. This book is both a lament for my father and a celebration of cakes. It is a story of loss and discovery.

Dad rose early six mornings a week to bake the bread and cakes for the tea shop and he typically worked fourteen-hour days. *Peter's* was my second home, where I grew up with my three siblings, Gordon, Johnny and Georgina (who we call Fuby). Our playground was our father's bakehouse, from where the scent of flour and cakes lingered on our clothes. Our toys were piping bags full of cream, and we played with pastry, rolled jam doughnuts in sugar and squished cream in meringue shells. The cake counters at the front of the tea shop, the tea room, customers and staff all formed a big part of our childhood. *Peter's* had a cosy, homely atmosphere. The café provided a haven for locals, who spent their time sipping tea and eating cakes and savouries. The visitors were varied: women with toddlers, school children, upper class Weybridge ladies, the occasional celebrity, priests, nuns, local shopkeepers, the wheelchair bound, couples in love and lonely souls. One tea shop reviewer said she half expected to see Miss Marple sipping tea in the corner. Some customers we knew by name, others by their favourite cake. I learned from a young age, when I was old enough to work there as a waitress, that tea and cake were always more than just fuel for the body; taking tea was an excuse to spend time with a friend or loved one, share stories, indulge in cakes and conversation (with not a mobile or laptop in sight in those days). Our tea room provided an escape from everyday life.

My mother, Frankie, a former nurse, was the face of the shop. She had a natural way with customers and was a surrogate mother to the boarders at nearby St George's College who came in for the daily College Tea: spaghetti or beans on toast with a poached egg followed by an iced bun or cream cake, a motherly chat and, if they were lucky, a lift back to school. The young boarders, who varied in ages, were regular customers, noticeable in their maroon blazers, while the pupils from St Maurs Convent made welcome appearances in their navy uniform with pretty straw boaters in summer. The premises had previously been a *Fuller's* tea room where my father had enjoyed coffee and walnut cake while a boarder at St George's from the ages of eight to eighteen (between 1939 and 1949).

IT MAY HAVE BEEN the seventies when I was growing up, but *Peter's* was in a time warp. It was a classic British café, with 1940s décor (rose floral wallpaper, small wooden tables, red cushioned chairs), a powder room and my father's motley collection of chamber pots lining the shelves. On the walls were paintings of Weybridge scenes alongside copper pans, decorative plates and a wall clock that chimed every quarter of an hour, as it had done for years in my grandparents' tea room, and as it does today in Mum's dining room.

I was aware from a young age that Nana and Papa, as I called my grandparents, had also run a tea shop, called *Lane's* in Westcliff near Southend, and my great-grandparents ran *Beti's* tea shop in Ryde on the Isle of Wight. My great-grandfather, Ferdinando, moved to Ryde from Marseille in 1886, aged nine, with his two brothers and mother, Maria, following the death of his father, Carlo. The family went to live with Maria's brother, Francois Beti, and his wife Mary, who ran *Beti's* tea room. Ferdinando eventually took over the running of this tea shop, where he worked as a pastry chef until his death in 1934. The business was then divided; my grandmother's two brothers, Charlie and Freddy, continued working at *Beti's*, while her other brother, Hector, later opened another tea shop, also called *Beti's*, in Southsea. My grandmother and grandfather opened *Lane's* in Westcliff, when Dad was three, which they ran until 1958, when they helped him set up *Peter's* in Weybridge. It seemed my father's role in life as a pastry chef was pretty much predetermined.

Growing up, I occasionally heard stories about our pastry chef ancestors coming from a small Swiss–Italian village, trudging across Europe to escape poverty, first to Marseille, France, where my great-grandfather was born, then to England, where they set up tea shops.

In 2000, *Peter's* closed. Dad was seventy and his health was in decline. Neither I nor my two brothers and sister had carried on the tradition. We all had our reasons. I had left the cosy confines of the cake shop to train as a journalist. But between visits I always missed my father's baking, the sight, scents and taste of homemade cakes, chocolates and savouries, plus the sound of machines whirring away in the bakehouse and customers chattering in the tea room. The closure of the tea shop signalled the end of generations of tea shops and bakers.

I soon discovered that it wasn't just the members of my family who were saddened by the closure of the shop. People wrote to say how much they missed their favourite treats: some mourned meringues, others missed the macaroons, many said they couldn't find a Welsh rarebit or chocolates like those my father made. Some people said the shop had been 'a friend' to them, others declared *Peter's* had a historical legacy because of the role it had played in the community for over forty years.

IT WAS ONLY WHEN I reached my forties that I started to ask more questions about my family's history. In 2005, I began researching and writing about our family tea shops. Why were there so many bakers and an obsession with tea, cake and homemade chocolates? Why did my parents open *Peter's*? And why on earth couldn't I bake?

This last question became more pressing when I had my children: Lara, now sixteen, and Joe, twelve. Over the years I had relied on my father to bake all the classic tea shop cakes for their birthday parties: the iced pink cottage cake for Lara, the chocolate train engine and fortress for Joe. As friends cooed over the birthday cakes, sometimes I omitted to say who had made them. I had taken it for granted that my father always made the cakes for every family occasion. I had had an excuse not to bake in my childhood because there simply had been no need to make cakes; life had revolved around the shop, where there had been a steady supply of 'homemade' sweet treats. But now I was a mother and the shop was closed, I realized that it was high time I learned to bake. Besides, an uncle once said that my father had chocolate and sugar flowing through his veins. I wondered if, perhaps, I might have inherited this magic baking gene, if only to discover it rather late in life.

My intention was to write a baking memoir based on my memories of a childhood growing up in a tea shop and the tales of our line of family pastry chefs, including recipes for all the classics. So, one day, while my father enjoyed his well-earned retirement at the family home in Weybridge, I turned up with a tape recorder and announced my plan. He looked perplexed. I started off by asking him about the family's pastry chef tradition. Peter went upstairs and returned with a green book, our family history, which I discovered traced our ancestors back to a village called Poschiavo on the Swiss–Italian border. This book, dusty from being hidden away for years, was self-published by Bernadette Forer, a distant relative in Canada, and contained details of my family lineage, including a family tree, photographs and stories. Entitled *The History and Genealogy of the Forer Family (1796–2002)*, it made fascinating reading about the overabundance of pastry chefs in Poschiavo and the mass emigration that followed. I discovered plenty of pastry chefs in my family, including not only my great-grandfather, Ferdinando, who ran *Beti's* on the Isle of Wight, but both his brothers, Joseph and Enrico, who also learned the art of baking pastries and managing tea shops. I was fascinated, but disappointed that I couldn't find a single recipe. When I asked Dad for copies of all the recipes for the tea shop cakes and pastries, I expected him to pop upstairs and return with a box load. Instead, he looked up with a quizzical expression and said, "They're all in my head. What do you want to know dear?" My mother put the kettle on, as she usually does in an emergency.

Admittedly, I had never seen Dad refer to any recipe books in the bakehouse, although I recalled bits of card with ingredient lists. After the heart-stopping moment of sheer panic when I realized there were no written recipes, I raided some of the boxes retrieved from *Peter's*, unopened since the shop closed in 2000, tucked away in a dusty corner of the attic. I came across some of the handwritten small cards, almost indecipherable, with names of cakes and ingredients in proportions that would blow your mind. Dad used these cards in the bakehouse, where he produced vast quantities of cakes for our customers. How could I be expected to mix forty pounds of flour in one go? How many eggs made a gallon? What would I do with two hundred and fifty Japonaise biscuits? These cards, smeared with the residues of jam and cream, formed the start of the Holy Grail. I found a mixture of recipe style cards and books but none contained recipes for the domestic cook. I describe the contents of these books as 'notes' as they often contained ingredients in large sizes without methods, as if written for a pastry chef working at one of the family tea shops producing big numbers of cakes.

I found a brown ledger full of neat handwriting that turned out to be the notes written by Peter's elder sister, my Aunty Hazell, who had grown up in *Lane's* tea shop alongside my father. I found another book or collection of notes, barely legible, without a cover, worn from age and nibbled at the edges, where the once-white paper had turned sepia. I originally thought this tattered notebook was my father's, but when I asked him to decipher a word he said it had belonged to his mother and was written in the heyday of her parents' tea shop, *Beti's*. As I flicked through the pages, some came loose in my hand, and they were infused with that telltale musty vanilla scent of both age and baking. Next, I found a hardback leather-bound indexed book made by Twinlock Crown (at a cost of one shilling) that, again, contained lists of ingredients in big proportions, but no methods. Some of the writing looked like Dad's, some like Aunty Hazell's and some resembled my grandmother's spidery scrawl. I came to the conclusion that my ancestors were more pastry chefs than writers. When I tried to make sense of these chaotic records I realized the enormity of the task ahead of me.

Initially, I tried to interview my father about the cakes and pastry chefs with a voice recorder, but I soon realized he was more comfortable baking than sitting still answering questions. It wasn't that long before he switched on the oven and suggested I get my hands messy. When it came to recording the tea shop recipes, one big challenge was to adapt the large shop quantities for the home cook. When I asked Dad for details on quantities, methods and cooking times his stock response was, "It's instinct and experience". While this was frustrating, it was the truth about Dad and the baker's life he led for over four decades, as well as his experience of watching all the bakers in his family work while he was growing up.

At first, I baked with my father so I could record the methods and put into practice the theory that was second nature to him. But I also wanted to chronicle his personal tips from a lifetime of baking. My children, Lara and Joe, came along and baked with us, too. Then my father held a few masterclasses in which my older brother, Johnny, and childhood friend, Karen, joined in. We

1

Peter's (Weybridge) Ltd.
27 CHURCH STREET · WEYBRIDGE · SURREY

Telephone: WEYBRIDGE 43282

VAT Registration No. 211

Coffee per cup.................	26p	Fruit juice...............	18p
Tea per pot...................	26p	Soup per portion.........	25p
China tea with milk or lemon.	28p	Omelettes.	
Chocolate per cup............	30p	Plain or savory..........	50p
Horlicks per cup.............	30p	Cheese, Ham, chicken	
Bovril per cup...............	28p	or mushroom.......	65p
Glass of milk................	20p	Poached egg on toast.....	50p
Orange or lemon drink per glass	12p.	Baked beans on toast....	50p
Coca cola or fants orange....	28p	Spaghetti on toast......	50p
Buns or doughnuts............	17p	Egg on beans or spaghetti	80p
Sausage roll.................	18p	Cheese and tomatoe flan.	50p
Cornish pasty................	22p	Welsh rarebit...........	60p
Toasted scone and butter.....	18p	Buck rarebit............	80p
Toasted tea cake and butter.	24p	Sardines on toast.......	50p
Toasted scone and butter,....	22p	Cornish pasty..........	22p.
Cakes served at the table....	2op	Cornish pasty with beans	
Fresh cream cakes at table..	26p	or spaghetti.....	58.
Bread and butter per portion.	16p.	Fresh cream and fruit pie	36p
Roll and butter..............	17p	Treacle tart and cream.	36p.
Plain roll...................	10p	Lemon meringue pie.....	35p.
Portion of butter............	7p.	Ice cream..............	22p.
Hot buttered toast...........	16p	Ice cream meringue.....	36p.
Jam per portion..............	10p	Cheese per portion,....	25p
Cream per portion............	20p	Cottage pie and peas....	85p.
Croissant and butter.........	18p.	Macaroni cheese........	80p.
Animal biscuits..............	18p.	Lasagne................	85p
Strawberry tart and cream..	26p.	Scotch egg.............	30p
Portion of strawberry flan.:	40p	Flan with beans and s	
Iced coffee..................	25p.	spaghetti..	60p
		Cheese roll............	22p.
		Ham or turkey roll.....	28p.

Salads. Sardine, cheese or egg.......... £1.10
    Ham or turkey................. £1.65.
    Scotch egg................... £1.40.
            Side salad..... 75p.
  Steak pie.... 45p.   Pate on toast.....65p.

ALL PRICES INCLUDE V.A.T.

1 *Peter's* menu, hand-typed on Dad's manual typewriter. 2 Dad in the bakehouse in the sixties, making coffee Japonaise. 3 *Peter's* exterior — my second home. 4 With Dad in County Wicklow, Ireland. 5 Mum with Dad behind the shop counter, holding one of his favourite chamber pots from the collection.

made everything from custard tarts to coffee Japonaise. It struck me after a few baking sessions that the recipes were simply part of my father, not just information held in his head.

As we baked, the stories about the cakes and tea shops flowed far more naturally than they did with me posing formal questions. I discovered that a wooden spoon, a mixing bowl and sweet cake ingredients were my best friends. My father was comfortable in my childhood kitchen teaching me to bake and sharing tales from the tea shops. When I baked my first loaf of white bread I was instantly back in the bakehouse, watching Dad knead the dough as he had done time and time again, before placing the large tray containing ten or so loaf tins in the oven. Handling the dough myself, with my father telling me to feel the consistency, was a revelation. I felt absorbed in baking bread and grateful that my dad was showing me how to do it. I was like a child again when the loaf came out of the oven and looked similar to the ones he had made. He tapped it on the base, teaching me to listen for the hollow sound to prove it was baked. My baking journey had begun.

EACH CAKE, SAVOURY PASTRY OR BREAD ROLL we made brought back a memory and a feeling linked to the tea shop, a customer, a member of staff, my family or an event. James Beard, the chef and food writer, said that 'taste memories' make life richer and, for me, this is certainly the case; every time I bit into one of our creations the taste sensation invariably led me back to my past. I remembered watching Dad knead dough, decorate cakes and make chocolates, and I recalled helping in the bakehouse, enjoying tea and cakes in the tea room with my friend Alice, holding my birthday parties in the café (friends thought I had the perfect childhood, growing up in a cake shop) and later working in the shop. But some memories filled me with sadness: tense visits from the Environmental Health Officer, the seemingly endless days my parents spent working in the shop, especially at Christmas and Easter, my father's collapse at work, the closure of the family business. I enjoyed the

> Each cake, savoury pastry or bread roll we made brought back a memory and a feeling linked to the tea shop, a customer, a member of staff, my family or an event.

companionship of baking with my father, but as time went on I sensed him slowing down as energy ebbed away from him. In the Spring of 2011, my father's health deteriorated further and I realized that time might be running out. While the baking was essential empirical research, it was proving both physically and mentally taxing for a weak elderly man. There were many medical investigations, the consultant ordered regular blood transfusions and Dad spent increasing amounts of time in hospital. Eventually, my father was no longer able to bake.

Peter's deterioration led to a role reversal whereby my mother, Frankie, rose to the challenge of regularly baking cakes and pastries under Peter's guidance as he sat on a stool in the kitchen. She did this naturally, keen to take part in the baking and in the knowledge that the scent, sight and taste of cakes made everyone happy. My brother Johnny stepped in to help make the jam doughnuts using the ancient jam machine we had played with as children. I finally made a birthday cake, Dad's favourite coffee and walnut cake, for his eightieth birthday on 29 April 2011. Lara and Joe began to excel at baking, too, with Lara revealing a natural talent for piping petals on cakes and adapting the traditional cakes from *Peter's* for her teenage friends. Joe followed his grandfather's lead by sprinkling chopped walnuts into carrot cake mix with surprising confidence and success. I felt the process had come full circle when Lara baked the pink cottage cake sponge for my niece's eighteenth birthday in October 2011 under the direction of her grandfather and with her uncle Johnny's help. The cake-making odyssey I set out upon became an unexpected bonding experience for my family, during which time we discovered that the baking gene lives on.

Whenever people heard about my baking lessons with my father, they asked me to share the recipes. Dad devoted his life to making sweet and savoury pastries and chocolates people loved. It seemed natural to share these in a cookbook to bridge the gap between my family's generations of baking experience and the contemporary home cook. I also wanted to tell the story of our tea shop through the recipes and stories about the cakes and some savouries Dad made. These simple recipes are suitable for all who share a passion for traditional cakes, both the beginner baker and the more experienced pastry chef. Included throughout are Peter's personal baking tips.

NOW, WHENEVER I MAKE CAKES I feel my father by my side again, urging me to 'bake with confidence and instinct'. I'm no longer afraid to get my hands messy. My initial obsession with finding and recording the recipes became far more than a recipe hunt. This rewarding experience gave me precious time with my father and mother. After we stopped baking Dad often asked me how my book was going. He said, "Don't forget to tell everyone how hard your mother worked; she was the shop." I promised to convey his message. The tea shop was founded on teamwork: Dad baked while Mum gave a warm welcome to everyone; Peter and Frankie offered a combination of homemade cakes, chocolates, conviviality and more.

My father's gift was to teach me not to feel tied to the written recipe. A good baker knows to trust their instinct – therein lies the magic in your hands. I hope you will follow the spirit of these recipes and share both the baking and the cakes with friends and family, creating your own taste memories to take with you into the future.

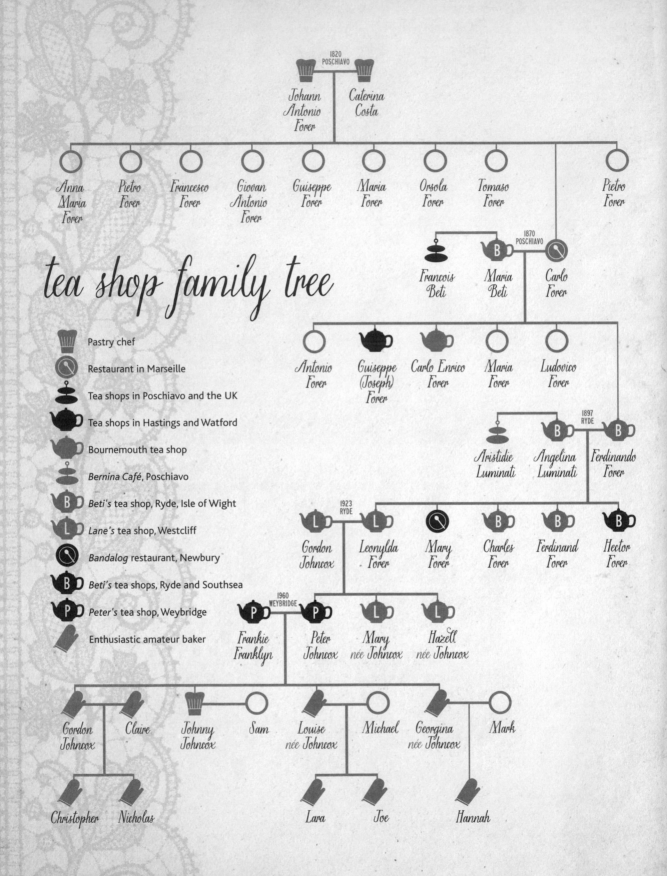

tea shop family tree

1820 POSCHIAVO
Johann Antonio Forer — Caterina Costa

Anna Maria Forer
Pietro Forer
Francesco Forer
Giovan Antonio Forer
Guiseppe Forer
Maria Forer
Orsola Forer
Tomaso Forer
Pietro Forer

Francois Beti
Maria Beti
1870 POSCHIAVO
Carlo Forer

Antonio Forer
Guiseppe (Joseph) Forer
Carlo Enrico Forer
Maria Forer
Ludovico Forer

Aristidie Luminati
Angelina Luminati
1897 RYDE
Ferdinando Forer

Gordon Johncox
Leonylda Forer
1923 RYDE
Mary Forer
Charles Forer
Ferdinand Forer
Hector Forer

Frankie Franklyn
1960 WEYBRIDGE
Peter Johncox
Mary née Johncox
Hazell née Johncox

Gordon Johncox
Claire
Johnny Johncox
Sam
Louise née Johncox
Michael
Georgina née Johncox
Mark

Christopher
Nicholas
Lara
Joe
Hannah

Legend

Pastry chef

Restaurant in Marseille

Tea shops in Poschiavo and the UK

Tea shops in Hastings and Watford

Bournemouth tea shop

Bernina Café, Poschiavo

Beti's tea shop, Ryde, Isle of Wight

Lane's tea shop, Westcliff

Bandalog restaurant, Newbury

Beti's tea shops, Ryde and Southsea

Peter's tea shop, Weybridge

Enthusiastic amateur baker

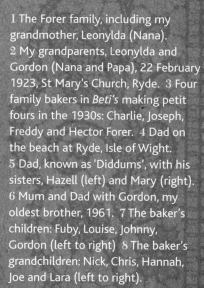

1 The Forer family, including my grandmother, Leonylda (Nana). 2 My grandparents, Leonylda and Gordon (Nana and Papa), 22 February 1923, St Mary's Church, Ryde. 3 Four family bakers in *Beti's* making petit fours in the 1930s: Charlie, Joseph, Freddy and Hector Forer. 4 Dad on the beach at Ryde, Isle of Wight. 5 Dad, known as 'Diddums', with his sisters, Hazell (left) and Mary (right). 6 Mum and Dad with Gordon, my oldest brother, 1961. 7 The baker's children: Fuby, Louise, Johnny, Gordon (left to right) 8 The baker's grandchildren: Nick, Chris, Hannah, Joe and Lara (left to right).

chapter one

The Baker's Little Helpers
Favourite Bakes for Children

Every Christmas and Easter, long after my childhood years, I would receive a box of chocolate peppermint creams, handmade by my father. The scent of sweet peppermint and bitter dark cocoa would hit me as I ran my eyes over the round-ridged chocolates in dark brown ruffled cases. Instantly, I'd be transported to the chocolate display cabinet in *Peter's*.

Suddenly, I'm ten years old, peering through a fringe of brown hair. I am sitting on a red-cushioned stool next to my younger sister, Fuby, who looks like a doll with her short brown hair and chocolate button eyes. We are folding white napkins and making up the white cake boxes inscribed in red with *Peter's*. We watch customers come and go from a table close to the counter in the tea room, we inhale the sweet scents and munch on animal biscuits.

There is a humming sound of conversation, rising and falling, and the clatter of cake forks in the tea room where customers enjoy afternoon tea: cream cakes, toasted teacakes, scones and other pastries. Macaroons, Madeira sponge, Battenberg and Florentines are some of the flavours of the day. Customers use white boned cake knives and forks to cut much anticipated pastries. Twinings loose-leaf tea is served in delicate china cups. For most people, afternoon tea conjures up tea, scones and clotted cream, but for me it is about the arrival of the glass stand containing eight cream cakes on a white doily, a meringue in the middle.

My mother, Frankie, captivates customers with her natural charisma, blind to her own charms. For one who works in a cake shop and has had four children, she is surprisingly slim. She is 'everyone's mother', as my brother Johnny puts it. Mum is always busy welcoming and serving.

A customer asks for four meringues. Mum goes to the fridge with a pair of silver-plated tongs and is careful not to crush the treat that loyal customers travel miles to taste.

My father Peter's place is in the bakehouse, where he practises his craft of making bread and cakes. His large rugby-player's hands knead the dough, day in, day out, his forearms twice the size of the average man's. Peter's trademark sideburns and thick head of wavy hair are always coated in a layer of flour. He smells of whatever he is making at the time – in the morning, Danish pastries and doughnuts, in the afternoon, the scent is of toasted teacakes and Welsh rarebit.

On Mondays, the day the shop closes, Dad makes chocolates, swapping his baker's white apron, smeared with ingredients, for his white chocolatier's coat with buttons down the front. My Great Uncle Charlie calls the process 'magic' as Dad conjures up exquisite chocolate creations from twenty-pound slabs of dark Belgian Callebaut chocolate. He sits on his stainless steel flour tin in front of his 'chocolate machine' – a metal container filled with molten chocolate. On the left side of the bench lie peppermint discs and the ancient dipping fork, a stainless steel instrument used to pick up the fondant sweet centres and sink them into the melted vat of chocolate. Dad dips his finger in the chocolate and licks; he has no thermometer or thermostat to measure it.

"How do you know it's ready?" I ask.

"Instinct and experience," he says.

Peter's greetings all involve invitations to eat: "Do you want something to eat darling?" Before I can answer he slips me a chocolate. I know from experience to accept or he will look dejected. Some fathers say, 'I love you'. My father gives me chocolates and cake.

MY CHILDHOOD MEMORIES are strongly shaped by the tea shop and Church Street, the small street on which it traded. I will never forget the yellow boxes of Cadbury's Flakes in the storeroom. In Peter's hands these became the thatched roof on my favourite pink cottage cake. Across the road was the newsagent, *Hayden's*, where I bought milk chocolate Curly Wurlies, not bitter like the dark chocolate from Belgium. Next door was *Haslets* haberdashery store, 'The Harrods of Weybridge', where I played hide and seek with my sister on three crammed floors. Frankie bought dressmaking patterns there and made most of our clothes on her Singer sewing machine.

Peter's was sandwiched between the *Midland Bank* and *Artistic Treasures*, an upmarket china shop run by Mr and Mrs Reece. Peter went there to buy presents for Frankie and Mr and Mrs Reece would often escape their business for tea and cake at *Peter's*.

The two most important shops were *Robson's*, the butcher on the High Street, and *Brockwell's*, the grocer's on Baker Street, where we bought fruit and vegetables. Peter's order for *Robson's* would include sausage meat for sausage rolls, ham for omelettes and minced meat for Cornish pasties and rissoles. Mum always gave me a bag of doughnuts to take to Mr Robson, a friendly

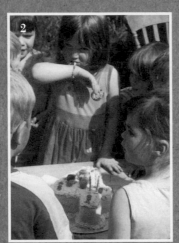

fellow with a moustache, who wore a blue-and-white striped apron. In return, he gave us spare bones for the bakehouse dog and occasional steaks. Gordon, my oldest brother, a chatterbox, worked there from the age of twelve. The exchange worked well: the butcher got a constant supply of cakes and some help, while the baker got cut-price meat and some peace. Whenever I saw Gordon at work he'd be yapping away to Mr Robson who often had a meat cleaver in hand; Gordon learnt how to pluck and gut chickens and make sausages. Why anyone would want to swap being in a cake shop for a stinky butcher's packed full of dead animals was a mystery to me. My other brother, Johnny, always helped in the bakehouse, rolling the jam doughnuts in sugar before cycling to school. One day, he came off his bike while eating a doughnut. Dad had bread in the oven so Johnny went in the ambulance alone. Mum, ever the nurse, rushed to the hospital afterwards while Peter ensured the bread didn't burn.

On Baker Street was a music shop run by a rotund gentleman with white hair called Horace Butler. My parents went there to buy me a guitar for my tenth birthday, plus *The New Beatles Complete*, a book that contained lyrics and guitar chords for songs recorded between 1967 and 1970: the soundtrack to my childhood.

Home was a three-bedroom semi a mile away from the tea shop. After a day in the bakehouse Peter's routine was to 'have a wash and a shave' before disappearing into his office in the loft to do 'the books'. The sound of Peter singing along to Edith Piaf's *Non, Je Ne Regrette Rien* floats down the stairs. Regrets? No, I don't think my father regretted being a baker and chocolatier.

THE RECIPES THAT FOLLOW are for the cakes and treats that I loved as a child – those that made the biggest impression on me during my formative years. And now, my own children enjoy them, too. Included is my favourite celebration cake, Peter's pink cottage cake.

SPONGE FINGERS

MAKES APPROXIMATELY 30

3 large eggs, separated

115g caster sugar

1 teaspoon vanilla extract

85g plain flour

½ teaspoon cream of tartar

1–2 tablespoons granulated sugar
(optional)

Dad made sponge fingers, the perfect treat for toddlers, once a week. When stressed mums came into the shop with a child crying, Mum quickly handed out a sponge finger and the noise instantly stopped. The only downside was the trail of crumbs left behind. Sponge fingers were also used for charlotte russe, which was made to order, and homemade trifles, which we served with a cherry on top in a small silver-plated dish.

Preheat the oven to 140°C/gas mark 1. Line 2 baking sheets with baking parchment.

Beat the yolks, sugar and vanilla extract together until the mixture is pale and creamy. Sift over the flour, but do not mix it in.

Whisk the whites with the cream of tartar until stiff peaks form. Gently fold the whites into the egg-and-flour mix.

Using a piping bag fitted with a plain 1cm nozzle, pipe a series of straight lines, roughly 10cm in length, onto the baking parchment, spacing them about 4cm apart. Sprinkle with a little granulated sugar, if desired.

Bake for 20 minutes or until the sponge fingers are golden brown and have some crunch.

baker's tip

Make sure that your sponge fingers are baked enough so that they snap, rather than tear, in half. If you can resist eating them all, save some for making a trifle or tiramisu.

FAIRY CAKES

MAKES 18

110g self-raising flour
110g butter, softened
110g caster sugar
2 eggs
1 teaspoon baking powder

FOR THE DECORATION

300g icing sugar
3–5 tablespoons water
Food colouring of your choice
Sprinkles

I grew up with good old-fashioned fairy cakes, not cupcakes or muffins. Dad made fairies (as he called them) for both the tea shop and for parties. And now my children enjoy making these fairies and decorating them with anything sweet. I would often raid Dad's storeroom for sprinkles, silver balls and chocolate flakes – it was a little girl's paradise.

Preheat the oven to 200°C/gas mark 6.

Mix all the cake ingredients together for 2–3 minutes until they are well blended and the mixture is smooth. Divide the mixture between 18 paper fairy cake cases. Bake on the top shelf of the oven for 15 minutes or until the cakes are risen and golden brown and an inserted skewer comes out clean. Cool on a wire rack.

To make the glacé icing, mix the icing sugar with enough water to make a paste. Add a few drops of the colour of your choice. Decorate the tops of the fairy cakes with the icing and as many sprinkles as you like.

baker's tip

You could decorate these cakes with buttercream instead of the icing, if you prefer. Fairy cakes are ideal for making with kids as they are easy to prepare and kids love to eat them. Young children can start off decorating with sprinkles and progress to piping intricate patterns and petals in icing as they gain experience and confidence.

ANIMAL BISCUITS

MAKES APPROXIMATELY 36 *

200g butter

200g caster sugar

2 eggs (or 1 egg, 1 yolk – you need 75g), beaten

400g plain flour, plus extra to dust

1 teaspoon baking powder

Pinch of salt

3–4 tablespoons apricot jam

2 x 500g coloured ready-to-roll icing

200g dark chocolate, broken into pieces

White royal icing, to decorate

* depending on the size of the cutter

We had fun decorating these chocolate-dipped animal biscuits with coloured icing and then piping eyes. Dad had cutters for various animal shapes, including a rabbit, penguin and chick, which was always popular at Easter. Fuby has these cutters now and still makes animal biscuits with her daughter, Hannah. Everyone enjoys making them, especially when a biscuit is accidentally submerged in the melted chocolate while dipping it.

Preheat the oven to 180°C/gas mark 4. Line a couple of baking sheets with baking parchment.

Cream the butter and sugar together until light and fluffy. Add the eggs, then stir in the flour, baking powder and salt. Gently but thoroughly mix to form a dough. Wrap the dough in cling film and chill it in the refrigerator for about 30 minutes.

Roll out the dough on a lightly floured surface to a thickness of 7mm. Using animal-shaped biscuit cutters, cut out your shapes. Reroll and use the trimmings for more biscuits. Transfer the shapes onto the prepared baking sheets and bake for 10–12 minutes until they are light brown. Leave the biscuits to cool on the baking sheet.

Meanwhile, gently heat the apricot jam in a small pan until warm or in a microwave for one minute until soft. Once they are cool, brush the surface of each biscuit with a small amount of warm apricot jam.

Roll out the icing to a thickness of about 2.5mm. Using the same cutters, cut out a corresponding icing shape for each biscuit and place it onto the biscuit over the warm jam. Set aside on the baking sheet.

baker's tip

Dad used a special patterned rolling pin to create a ribbed effect on the icing for these animal biscuits. You can buy a textured rolling pin or a patterned mat from good kitchen shops if you would like to create a surface pattern in the icing.

Melt the chocolate in a bowl set over a pan of simmering water, then take the bowl off the pan. To dip each biscuit, place it on a fork, put a finger from the other hand on top to steady the biscuit and dip it into the chocolate so that its base and sides are covered. As you lift the biscuit out of the bowl, drag it against the side of the bowl to remove excess chocolate. Place it on a piece of baking parchment, chocolate-side down, to set. When the chocolate has set, the parchment paper will peel off easily, leaving the chocolate behind on the biscuit.

Once the chocolate has set, pipe white royal icing to make the whites of the eyes. Use a cocktail stick to dab some melted chocolate onto the white icing to form pupils.

TRAFFIC LIGHT BISCUITS

MAKES 20–22

200g butter

200g caster sugar

2 eggs (or 1 egg, 1 yolk – you need 75g), beaten

400g plain flour, plus extra to dust

1 teaspoon baking powder

Large pinch of salt

Approximately 10 tablespoons apricot jam or plain piping jelly

Icing sugar, to dust

Red, yellow and green food colouring

When children came into the tea shop they immediately pointed to these traffic light biscuits behind the counter with their jewel-like red, orange and green 'lights'. Mums often bought them for a quick treat for their child and these biscuits always guaranteed to brighten up any birthday party table. They are also fun and messy to make.

Preheat the oven to 180°C/gas mark 4. Line a couple of baking sheets with baking parchment.

Follow the instructions for making biscuit dough on page 26.

Roll out the dough on a lightly floured surface to a thickness of about 5mm. Using an 8cm oval cutter, cut out 40–44 ovals. If you have not got an oval cutter, cut the dough into 9.5 x 3.5cm rectangles.

On half of the biscuits, use a small round cutter (approximately 1.5cm) to cut a row of 3 evenly spaced holes along each biscuit. Transfer all the biscuits to the prepared baking sheets and bake for 10–12 minutes or until the biscuits are lightly golden brown.

Meanwhile, gently heat the apricot jam in a small pan until warm or in a microwave for 1 minute until soft.

Allow the biscuits to cool, then sandwich them together with warm apricot jam, with plain biscuits at the bottom and 3-holed biscuits on top. Sift icing sugar over the biscuit tops. Do not use too much icing sugar (a light dusting will do) otherwise your coloured jam will not stick inside the cut-out circles.

Divide the remaining jam into 3 equal portions. Colour 1 portion with 4 drops of red food colouring, 1 portion with 4 drops of yellow and the final portion with 4 drops of green. Spoon a blob of each coloured jam into a hole on the top of each biscuit, positioning the colours in traffic light order.

the baker's little helpers

JAM TARTS

MAKES 15–18

200g plain flour, plus extra to dust
125g butter, plus extra for greasing
75g caster sugar
40g egg (approximately 1 egg), beaten
Assorted jams (allow 1 teaspoonful
    per tart)

Jam tarts always remind me of birthday parties. The tables in the tea room were rearranged down the centre and groaned under the weight of treats: jam tarts, lemon tarts, chocolate cornflake cakes, animal biscuits, fairy cakes, little sandwiches, mini sausage rolls, cheese on sticks, jelly, ice cream and chocolate blancmange. We held parties on a Sunday or Monday afternoon, but customers often tried to sneak in. Some even gate-crashed and sat down for tea.

Preheat the oven to 180°C/gas mark 4. Grease the tart tins.

Rub together the flour and butter in a bowl until the mixture resembles fine cake crumbs.

Add the egg to the caster sugar and mix them together – this allows the sugar grains to dissolve into the egg so that the sugar is evenly distributed throughout the pastry. Add the egg-and-sugar mix to the flour mixture, then knead them together to form a dough. Wrap the dough in cling film and place in the refrigerator for 30 minutes.

Roll out the pastry on a floured surface to a thickness of about 5mm. Using a round pastry cutter, cut out circles that are slightly bigger than the holes in your jam tart tins. Gently press the circles into the holes in the tins. The remaining pastry can be rolled out and used again, but bear in mind that it will become slightly tougher with each rolling.

Carefully place a good teaspoonful of jam into each pastry case. Bake for approximately 15 minutes or until the pastry is golden brown. Leave the tarts to cool in the tins for about 5 minutes, until the jam has set, then transfer them to a wire rack to cool completely.

baker's tip

Lemon curd tarts are also tasty and, if you use lemon curd as well as an assortment of flavoured jams, you'll create a colourful display that's perfect for children's parties.

CHOCOLATE CRUNCH

MAKES 25

300g plain or milk chocolate, broken
  into small pieces

150g butter, plus extra for greasing

230g digestive biscuits

90g icing sugar

Smarties, to decorate

We used to make this at home when I was a child and I still make it today for family parties. Chocolate crunch takes me back to *Charlie's Angels*. We would munch on the crunch while watching this classic seventies' American TV drama – I pictured myself as Sabrina Duncan. Chocolate crunch is always best served with Smarties on top.

Grease an 18cm shallow square cake tin.

Melt the chocolate and butter in a bowl set over a pan of simmering water. Stir the butter and chocolate together over the heat until they are well blended.

Meanwhile, crumble the biscuits into a mixing bowl (you want peanut-sized pieces). Sift in the icing sugar and mix it into the biscuit crumble. Pour the chocolate mixture over the biscuit pieces and mix thoroughly.

Press the mixture into the tin and level off the surface with a palette knife. Using a knife, score the surface into 25 squares. Place Smarties on top while the mixture is still soft, pressing them into the surface so they will stick. Chill in the refrigerator for 1 hour to set. Turn the mixture out of the tin and, using your score marks to guide you, cut the squares with a knife.

baker's tip

If you're not a fan of Smarties you can decorate chocolate crunch with other sweets, such as chocolate buttons (ordinary or coloured), M&Ms or mini marshmallows. Squares of chocolate crunch, sealed in bags tied with ribbon, always make a lovely gift.

the baker's little helpers

CHOCOLATE CORNFLAKE CAKES

MAKES 20

100g butter
400g dark or milk chocolate
160g cornflakes

Dad made huge vats of chocolate-coated cornflake cakes. He always used Kellogg's Cornflakes and dark Belgian Callebaut chocolate. One of my favourite jobs was mixing the chocolate and flakes then spooning into the paper cake holders. Most people have memories of making these crispy cakes at home with their mum. I made them with Dad using three pints of molten chocolate and three packets of cornflakes.

Melt the butter and chocolate in a bowl over a saucepan on a low heat. Pour the chocolate over the cornflakes in a bowl. Stir all the ingredients using a wooden spoon until all of the flakes are coated. Spoon the mixture into about 20 cake cases. Place in the fridge to set.

baker's tip

You can swap cornflakes for Rice Krispies. Split the mixture in half and add 4 teaspoons of golden syrup to one half to make a sticky texture. Top with sweets or decorations of your choice.

SWISS BUNS

MAKES 6-8

7g dried yeast or 21g fresh yeast

40g sugar

1 teaspoon milk

125ml warm water

300g strong white bread flour, plus extra to dust

¼ teaspoon salt

40g chilled butter, cubed

½ egg (you need 25g), beaten

Vegetable oil, for greasing

SWISS BUN ICING

2 tablespoons warm water

225g icing sugar

These soft finger-shaped buns were iced with pink, vanilla or chocolate icing in the tea shop. On special occasions, Dad made big orders of the Swiss buns for Rosslyn House, a finishing school based in the nearby village of Oatlands. On delivery days, I sat squashed in the boot of our green Hillman Hunter beside the trays of buns and other pastries.

Put the yeast, 1 teaspoon of the sugar and the milk into the warm water and leave to ferment for about 10 minutes. Line a baking sheet with baking parchment.

Mix together the flour, remaining sugar and salt. Rub in the butter.

When the yeast mixture is ready (when it appears risen and frothy), add it to the flour mixture. Blend in the egg until the ingredients are combined and you have a soft dough. Turn out the dough onto a lightly floured surface and knead for about 10 minutes until the dough is smooth and elastic. Place it in a lightly oiled bowl, cover with oiled cling film and leave the dough to rise in a warm place for 1½–2 hours until it has doubled in size.

Turn out the risen dough onto a lightly floured surface and knock it back. Divide it into 70g pieces and roll each piece into a sausage shape about 13cm in length. Place these onto the prepared baking sheet, spacing them about 3cm apart. (Alternatively, divide the dough into 8 equal pieces and roll each piece into a sausage shape.) Leave the dough pieces uncovered in a warm place for about 30–40 minutes until they have doubled in size. Preheat the oven to 190°C/gas mark 5.

Bake for 12–15 minutes or until the buns are light brown and soft to the touch. Then transfer the buns to a wire rack and leave to cool.

Gradually add the water to the icing sugar to form a smooth, thick consistency. Then dip the top of each bun into the icing. Smooth out the surface with a palette knife, removing excess icing as you go. Leave the iced buns on a wire rack to allow the icing to set.

baker's tip
You can use fondant instead of icing, or colour and/or flavour the icing according to your choice.

PINK COTTAGE CAKE

This is my favourite childhood birthday cake. Dad made it for me most birthdays and the tradition continued when he made it for my daughter, Lara. I loved the chocolate flakes as the roof, the pink iced walls, the pretty garden and pond. My niece, Hannah, requested this cake for her eighteenth birthday in October 2011. Dad was too ill to bake, but he gave instructions for us to make it just as he had so many times.

SERVES 20–25

FOR THE VANILLA SPONGE

450g caster sugar

1 teaspoon salt

450g butter

12 medium eggs (you need 630g), beaten

700g self-raising flour

1 teaspoon vanilla extract

FOR THE DECORATION

400g butter, softened

400g icing sugar, sifted, plus extra to dust

¾ teaspoon vanilla extract

200g jar mixed fruit jam (confectionery jam)

650g white ready-to-roll icing

Food colouring in pink, green and blue

Approximately 7 tablespoons cocoa

10–16 chocolate flakes

Preheat the oven to 150°C/gas mark 2. Line a 20cm square cake tin, with a depth of approximately 6cm, with baking parchment.

Make the sponge. Cream the sugar, salt and butter together. Gradually add the whisked eggs, mixing continually. Add the flour one-fifth at a time until it is fully combined, then add the vanilla extract. Gently pour the mixture into the prepared cake tin, ensuring it is evenly spread.

Place the tin on a baking sheet and bake for 1 hour, then check to ensure it is not becoming too brown – you may need to cover the tin with baking parchment if the top of the sponge is browning too much. Place the tin back in the oven and bake for a further ½ hour or until a skewer inserted into the centre of the cake comes out clean. Allow to cool in the tin.

Make the buttercream. Cream together the butter, icing sugar and vanilla extract for 5–10 minutes or until the mixture is thick, smooth and creamy. The mixture should be thick enough to stick firmly to a vertical surface without sliding off.

TRIMMING AND SLICING THE SPONGE

Once the sponge has cooled, remove it from the tin. It will be roughly 6cm tall. You now need to cut the top third of the sponge (which is roughly 2cm deep) to create the roof shape and remove any hard crust (the lower two-thirds will form the walls below the roof). Using a large knife, cut the top third to form a gentle sloping pyramid shape. Now gently cut the sides of the sponge to both ensure a flat surface and to remove any crisp sponge. You now have the basis of the cottage shape. Cut the sponge into 3 equal horizontal layers, each about 2cm deep. Separate the layers carefully.

PREPARING THE SPONGE FOR ICING

Leaving the base layer on the work surface, spread a generous covering of jam over it, then return the middle layer of sponge on top. Now spread a generous layer of buttercream onto the middle layer of sponge before returning the top (roof) layer on top. Place 4 tablespoons of the vanilla buttercream in a bowl and set aside for decorating the flowerbed and pond border. Keep the remaining buttercream for the roof and flowerbeds.

the baker's little helpers

ICING THE SPONGE

Take 300g of the white ready-to-roll icing and gently knead it to soften it. Mix it with enough pink food colouring to create a vibrant mid-pink icing.

Dust the pink icing and work surface (you will need a good metre of surface clear) with icing sugar and roll the icing under the palms of your hands to form a sausage shape. Continue rolling to slowly extend the sausage to around 80cm in length. Using a textured rolling pin, carefully flatten out the icing until it is the depth of a two-pound coin and wide enough to reach up the sides of the cake.

Apply a generous layer of the buttercream around the sides of the cake. Now it's time to apply pink icing to the sides of the sponge, over the buttercream, to represent the walls of the cottage. Cut the strip of pink icing into 4 pieces, one for each wall, and stick the pieces, one at a time, to the buttercream that you applied to the sides of the sponge. Smooth down the icing along the joins between finger and thumb for a neat finish. Alternatively, if you are feeling confident, roll 1 long strip of pink icing to go all around the sides of the cake and apply that to the buttercream on the walls of the cottage, thus avoiding corner joins. Set aside the excess pink icing (you'll use this to make the chimneys and chimneystack) and buttercream (you'll need that for the flowers in the flowerbeds).

Now carefully lift the sponge and fix it to the back-left corner of a 30cm cake board. Use a few dollops of buttercream to stick it to the board.

Mix the buttercream you had set aside for the roof and flowerbeds with 3–4 tablespoons cocoa to produce a rich dark brown cream. Apply two-thirds of this chocolate buttercream to the roof area of the cottage, being careful not to let it overspill onto the pink walls. Reserve the remaining chocolate buttercream for the flowerbeds.

CREATING INDIVIDUAL FEATURES IN ICING

Take 200g of the remaining white ready-to-roll icing and knead it until it is soft. Add enough green colouring to produce a light green colour for the lawn area. Roll out the green icing to the depth of a two-pound coin. Cut it to fit on the cake board around the cottage, then carefully lift it into position, dabbing a small amount of water onto the board to keep the lawn in place. Trim the icing at the edges of the board to produce a clean finish.

Using a sharp knife, cut away a 15mm band of green icing from around the edge of the cottage to create a gap that will form a flowerbed. Cut away another band of green icing of a similar width that leads from the edge of the board to the front door – this will form a path. Using a round biscuit cutter, cut away 2 circles of green icing to the front of the cottage, on either side of the path – 1 will become a flower bed, the other, a pond.

Take 75g of the remaining white ready-to-roll icing and knead it until it is soft. Add enough blue food colouring to create a pale blue colour. Roll this out to the depth of a one-pound coin. Using the back of a knife, score the icing in a series

the baker's little helpers

of close parallel lines. Then do the same at an angle across the existing lines in order to create a diamond lattice pattern. Now cut the blue icing into 4 rectangles to form the windows of your cottage – if you like you can make the windows for the sides of the cottage slightly longer than those at the front, as Peter did. Fix 2 rectangles to the front of the cottage, on either side of the front door, using a small amount of water to stick them to the pink icing, then attach a window on each of the 2 sides of the cottage.

With the remaining blue icing, add some more of the blue colouring to create a darker blue colour. Roll this out to the depth of a two pound coin and, using the same round biscuit cutter you used to create circles in the lawn for the flowerbed and pond, cut out a round piece of blue icing. Place this into 1 of the cut-out sections of lawn and there is your pond. Using either a very fine paintbrush or a cocktail stick, carefully draw small wavy lines of the undiluted blue food colouring across the pond to represent ripples in the water.

Now make the shutters that will go on either side of the windows. Take another 75g of the remaining white ready-to-roll icing and knead it until it is soft. Gradually add 2 tablespoons cocoa to create a mid-brown colour. Roll out the icing to the depth of a one-pound coin. Use the back of a knife to gently score the icing in a series of parallel lines to create a slatted-wood effect. Now cut out 8 small rectangles to the same height as the windows and the width you feel looks right for shutters. Stick the shutters to the pink walls on either side of the windows, using a very small amount of water to fix them in place.

Make the door using leftover brown icing from the shutters. Gently score the icing with the back of a knife to create a ribbed effect, then cut a rectangle that you feel is a good size for the door of your cottage, ensuring the ribbed effect runs along the length of the door. Fix the door in place at the centre of the front wall of the cottage using a small amount of water to attach it to the pink icing.

To the remaining brown icing add a little more cocoa to create a darker brown colour. You will use this for the footpath that leads from the edge of the board to the front door of the cottage. Roll this out to the depth of a two-pound coin. Using the back of a knife, score lines to create the effect of cobblestones on the surface of the icing. Carefully cut the brown icing to fit the space on the board that you left for the path. Again, use a small amount of water to fix the icing to the cake board.

To make the chimneystack, take some of the remaining pink ready-to-roll icing and mould it into the size and shape of a matchbox (make it roughly 4 x 2cm). Use the back of a knife to score a brick pattern on the large sides and ends of the chimneystack. Secure this to the top of the roof with a little water. Take 2 marble-sized pieces of pink icing and gently roll them to form 2 barrels. Take a pencil-sized piece of dowel (or use a pencil or cotton bud) and push it into the centre of each barrel from 1 end to form 2 chimneys. Gently push the chimneys onto the top of the chimneystack, again using a very small amount of water to stick them in place.

WORKING ON THE ROOF

To create the thatched roof, place 1 flake along each of the roof ridges. Carefully arrange the remaining flakes across the roof, side by side, ensuring there are no gaps between them. You will need to cut the flakes to size with a finely serrated knife. The flakes should slightly overhang the sides of the roof. Depending upon which flakes you have bought, you may find that, individually, they are too thick or disproportionately large. If this is the case, cut the flakes along their length to form a thinner thatch. Don't worry about the ones that break – you can fit them in across the roof (or, failing that, you can always just eat the excess). It is inevitable that some pieces of flake will fall from the roof, so once you have finished placing the flakes, it is best to gently brush away any broken pieces.

FINISHING OFF

Place the remaining chocolate buttercream into a piping bag and, using a 2–3mm nozzle, pipe parallel lines of chocolate buttercream around the cottage, into the area from which you previously cut away green icing, to create a flowerbed. Starting in the centre of the cut-out circle in the lawn, pipe concentric circles to create another flowerbed.

Take the remaining white butter icing and, using a 2–3mm nozzle, pipe small blobs of icing along the flowerbeds around the cottage to create white flowers Also, pipe about 8 white blobs in the flowerbed on the lawn to represent flowers. If you are confident, you can also place a blob on both the front door and the shutters to represent handles. As an added touch you can pipe around the pond and flowerbed and on either side of the footpath.

Place the jam in a piping bag and, using a 1–2mm nozzle, pipe a small bead onto the top of each of the white blobs to form red flowers.

Finally, take 2 small pieces of cotton wool and gently tease out the strands in one direction until each piece of cotton wool is almost transparent. Flatten each piece between the palms of your hand, then gently place one edge into each of the chimney pots to simulate smoke escaping from the chimney, using the back of your piece of dowel to gently force the cotton wool into place. Ensure both pieces tail away at the same angle, as if caught in the wind. Your pink cottage cake is now ready to serve.

the baker's little helpers

JAM DOUGHNUTS

MAKES 10

225g bread flour

Pinch of salt

50g margarine

15g fresh yeast or 2 level teaspoons dried yeast and 2 teaspoons caster sugar

5 tablespoons tepid water

1 egg

Vegetable oil, for deep frying

Approximately 4 tablespoons jam

Fine caster sugar, for coating

Injecting jam into round doughnuts was one of the best bakehouse jobs. Once jammed, we rolled the doughnuts in sprinkled sugar, which Dad laid out on copies of *The Daily Telegraph*. One day, my granddad, Papa, played a trick on Jack, a local allotment holder, when he injected English mustard into a doughnut. When Jack bit into it he turned bright red and spat it out. A smooth jam filling goes down much better!

Sift the flour and salt into a mixing basin and then rub in the margarine. Set aside.

If using fresh yeast, blend it with the tepid water. If using dried yeast, stir the sugar into the tepid water, then sprinkle in the yeast and stir together until both the sugar and yeast are dissolved. Set this mixture aside in a warm place until frothy – this takes about 10 minutes.

Mix the egg into the yeast liquid, then pour the mixture into the centre of the dry ingredients and mix to form a soft dough. Knead thoroughly by hand for 2–3 minutes. Place in a greased bowl and cover the dough. Set it aside in a warm place for about 45 minutes or until the dough has doubled in size.

Turn out the dough onto a lightly floured surface and knead it gently. Divide it into 10 equal pieces. Flatten each one slightly to form more of a disc shape than a ball. Place the balls of dough on a tray, cover and leave in a warm place for about 30 minutes until they are puffy looking.

baker's tip

Instead of filling the doughnuts with jam, try using crème pâtissière or pulped stewed apple. Also, you could try dipping your doughnuts into melted chocolate.

Heat the oil in a deep-fat fryer or a medium-sized deep saucepan. Fry 1 doughnut to test the temperature of the fat, which should instantly boil around the dough. If the oil is bubbling away nicely, add the remaining doughnuts. Cook for about 4 minutes until the doughnuts are golden brown, then carefully turn each doughnut once with a palette knife in order to reveal a golden-brown cooked side. Cook for 1–2 minutes on this side until golden brown. Remove each doughnut from the oil and allow the oil to drain from it, then place the doughnuts on kitchen paper to drain.

Once they are cool, use a piping bag fitted with a fine nozzle to inject about 1 teaspoon of jam into the centre of each doughnut. Alternatively, you can use a kitchen syringe or even a turkey baster, although I don't recommend injecting jam into your turkey at Christmas.

Roll the doughnut in fine caster sugar.

the baker's little helpers

FRESH CREAM FINGER DOUGHNUTS

To make fresh cream finger doughnuts, follow the method for making the doughnut dough. Roll the dough under the palm of your hand to create a sausage-shape. Prove and cook as per the recipe. Then drain and cool the doughnuts, roll them in fine caster sugar and cut along the centre lengthwise. Cut three-quarters of the way through, taking care not to separate each half. Bear in mind that if you do not cut deep enough, each half will close like a clam and cream will be forced out when you take a bite. Pipe a bead of jam the thickness of a pencil along the base of the cut, then pipe some fresh cream along the length of the doughnut.

SCOTCH PANCAKES

MAKES APPROXIMATELY 20

250g plain flour
25g caster sugar, plus extra to serve
½ teaspoon bicarbonate of soda
1 teaspoon cream of tartar
1 large egg
285g milk
2 tablespoons vegetable oil
Butter, to serve

Also known as drop scones, Scotch pancakes were one of the first sweet things we helped Dad to make in the shop. We would ladle the batter onto the special griddle and flip over the pancake with delight to see, hey presto, the tasty-looking cooked side! On Shrove Tuesday, Dad's Uncle Freddy, a widower who had worked in Beti's tea room as a chef, came into the shop and made the traditional pancakes for the café. Customers rarely stopped at just one.

Sift the flour and dry ingredients into a large mixing bowl. Make a well in the centre, break in the egg and pour in half the milk. Mix the ingredients with a balloon whisk from the centre, gradually incorporating the flour. Beat in the remaining milk and 1 tablespoon of the oil. The consistency should be similar to that of thick yogurt.

Heat a flat frying pan or griddle over a medium heat. Use some of the remaining vegetable oil to lubricate the surface of the pan. Now drop 1 tablespoon of the batter onto the griddle or pan to form a circle with a diameter of about 8cm and cook. When little holes appear, turn over the pancake with an egg slice. Cook until the underside is lightly brown. Make sure you don't overcrowd the pan if cooking more than 1 pancake at a time. Repeat until you've used all the batter. Serve hot with a knob of butter.

chapter two

When Peter Met Frankie
Love on a Plate

A tea shop would have been a natural place for Peter to have met Frankie, but it didn't happen that way. When Peter wasn't baking at his parents' tea shop, *Lane's*, in Westcliff, he was playing rugby or relaxing at Southend Rugby Club where he was the captain. On Saturday nights the club was always packed with raucous players and, on this occasion in the autumn of 1957, a big group of nurses had arrived for the Saturday night dance. The rugby team had won their match and the drinks were flowing. Over in one corner, a drunken group sang rugby songs, arms flung around each other.

That night, Frankie was in the club with her nurse friend, Bev. Frankie had moved from East London to work at a children's convalescent home in Southend before training to be a nurse at Southend General Hospital.

Peter, who was with his friend Jack, had spotted Frankie among the crowd: slim with short dark wavy hair, wearing a blue striped v-neck dress with a full skirt that was fitted with a belt, which showed off her tiny waist. Jack had his eye on Bev who had curly blonde hair and wore a red dress.

As Jack approached the nurses he gave Peter a nudge. "Hello ladies," he smiled. "May we introduce ourselves?"

Bev laughed. "Here we go… looks like we've got a right pair!" She exchanged a knowing glance with Frankie.

"My name is Jack and…" There was an awkward pause. Bev nodded at Peter. "Has he lost his tongue, then?"

"This is the captain, Peter. He's the strong, silent type!"

"Well, I never, the captain! My name's Bev and this is Frankie."

"Hello!" Peter offered to shake the nurses' hands. Frankie smiled.

"Pleased to meet you." She noticed that Peter was quite posh, dressed smartly in beige cavalry twill trousers and brown suede brothel creepers. Jack nudged Peter harder.

"Great music tonight, isn't it?" Jack tapped his leg.

"Yeah," Bev joined in the fun.

"Shall we dance then? You've got the legs for it!" Jack said.

"Cheeky boy!" Bev patted her hair. "You two have been staring at us all night. We wondered if you were ever going to come over." Jack and Bev looked pointedly at Peter who cleared his throat.

"Sorry, would you like to dance?" he asked Frankie.

"If you're sure." Frankie was embarrassed, aware that Peter had needed someone else to goad him on.

"Sorry about my friend. He's a bit slow off the mark," said Jack. Bev led the way to the dance floor with the two men and Frankie close behind.

"I'm afraid I've got two left feet," Peter warned Frankie.

"It's not a dance competition!" Frankie reassured him. Bev grabbed Jack by the hand and led him to the centre of the dance floor. As Peter took Frankie in his arms he noticed her blue eyes.

"Are you from around here?" he asked.

"I'm from the East End. I came to Southend to train to be a nurse. Are you from Westcliff then?"

"I was born on the Isle of Wight, but live locally."

"What do you do?"

"My parents run a bakery and tea shop. It's been in the family since 1934."

"That's nice, sounds like it keeps you busy. What's it called?"

"*Lane's*. It's hard work, but I'm my own boss, and it's all I've ever known."

"What kind of cakes do you make?" she asked.

"Traditional cakes. What's your favourite?"

"I like Eccles cakes."

"Well, I can certainly make you some Eccles."

"Really? That would be kind." Frankie smiled. A slow song struck up and Peter pulled her closer to him. Frankie was taken aback by this show of confidence. They danced cheek to cheek for a minute. Peter's trademark sideburns tickled Frankie's face. He inhaled her rose-scented perfume.

A few days after the dance, Peter was true to his word and arrived at Frankie's digs clutching a bag containing some Eccles cakes. Frankie had grown up with rationing during the war years. She

had been evacuated from East London to Somerset when she was just three. Her mother died when she was nine. No-one had ever made her a cake. She opened the bag and inhaled. "These smell wonderful. I'll put the kettle on."

This is how my parents described how they met, with every detail preserved in the retelling of this story. After the dance they said they dated for a while but lost touch. Dad had been busy setting up Peter's, which opened in Weybridge on 10 December 1958. Mum finished her nurse's training and worked in London as a theatre sister for some time. Falling in love so young wasn't in either of their plans.

After a bout of miserable weather in London, Mum decided to pack up her life and emigrate to Australia on a £10 ticket with two of her nurse friends. British nurses were in demand in Australia and Mum told me that the Australian doctors at Southend General Hospital had sown the seed by describing a sunny, laid-back lifestyle in Oz. Besides, she had not heard from Dad for some time and wanted more out of life than long nursing shifts in London and an uncommitted beau. When Dad finally discovered Mum's plans, her ship was about to sail and her trunk was already on board. In a mad scramble of a journey, he made it to the dockside, thanks to Jack driving him through the night all the way from Weybridge to Tilbury docks.

Dad took Mum for a cup of tea in a last ditch attempt to convince her of his love. He knew this was his big chance. He looked deeply into her eyes. Or he tried to, anyway. She stared out of the window towards the sea, to avoid his earnest gaze.

"Don't go, Frankie. Let's get married and live together."

He leaned forward and kissed her cheek, just by her ear. And then he whispered, "Will you give it all up to be with me?"

And she did. That was the whole miracle of it. She did.

THAT FIRST HOMEMADE ECCLES CAKE helped to bring Frankie and Peter together. Over the years, whenever Dad made Eccles cakes he always gave one, fresh from the oven, to Mum. The following recipes all follow the theme of love tokens – a perfect sweet treat for someone you love.

love on a plate

ECCLES CAKE

MAKES APPROXIMATELY 6

250g puff pastry (see recipe on
    page 132) or use shop-bought

25g butter

1 tablespoon light brown sugar

90g currants

25g mixed peel, finely chopped

¼ teaspoon ground cinnamon

¼ teaspoon ground ginger

¼ teaspoon allspice

Caster sugar, to sprinkle

Being the cake that cemented Mum and Dad's blossoming relationship, the Eccles cake remains one of Mum's favourites. At first, I feared these would be hard to make, but once you have mastered the art of making puff pastry (or simply buy some) the filling is easy. Dad was a great believer in a generous sprinkling of sugar. I've bought Mum different variations over the years but mass produced Eccles cakes just don't taste the same.

Preheat the oven to 200°C/gas mark 6.

Cream the butter and brown sugar together. Add the currants, mixed peel and spices.

Cut the pastry into 6 circles that are approximately 12cm in diameter. Place a couple of teaspoons of the filling mixture onto the centre of each circle. Fold the outer edges of each circle into the centre, working from opposite ends and gently depressing the edges into the middle. Once complete, turn over each circle so that the smooth side is facing up.

Using a rolling pin, gently roll each disc in order to flatten it to approximately 1cm in depth. Brush with a little water and sprinkle with caster sugar. Make 2 or 3 cuts on the top of each cake. Put the cakes on a baking sheet and bake for 25–30 minutes or until golden brown.

baker's tip

Peter added mixed peel to give these cakes an added zest flavour.

when Peter met Frankie

FRUIT SCONES

MAKES 10

525g self-raising flour, plus extra
to dust

90g cold butter, cut into sugar-
lump-sized cubes

90g caster sugar

90g sultanas (or your choice of
dried fruit)

300ml milk, plus extra for glazing

1 teaspoon vanilla extract

There were always trays of scones in the cake cabinet and in the tea room. Tea and homemade scones – the bread and butter of a tea shop. Dad made variations of scones: plain white, fruit, wholemeal and cheese. The sweet varieties were served with butter, homemade jam and clotted cream or Jersey cream. Scones were best eaten the day they were baked. The next day, they could be toasted and, on the third day, broken into crumbs and used to make treacle tart.

Preheat the oven to 200°C/gas mark 6. Line a baking tray with baking parchment and dust it with flour.

Sift the flour into a bowl and, using your fingertips, rub in the butter. Once the mixture resembles fine breadcrumbs and all the butter has been rubbed in (if you give the bowl a good shake, any remaining large lumps should rise to the surface), you can stir in the caster sugar and sultanas.

Put the milk and vanilla extract into a jug and gradually add this into the flour mixture, stirring gently after each addition; you may not need it all – you are looking for dough that is slightly sticky to the touch but it shouldn't be swimming in milk.

Flour your work surface and scrape the scone mixture onto it. Dust your rolling pin generously with flour and roll out the scone mixture until it is roughly 2cm thick. Using a 7cm pastry cutter, cut out 10 scones and place them on the prepared baking sheet. Glaze the scones with milk, then bake for 15–20 minutes or until golden brown.

baker's tip

Peter used the milk that had been boiled for making coffees the previous day in these scones, along with any whipped cream he might have had left over, as substitutes for some of the milk in this recipe. This made the scones taste rich and creamy.

love on a plate

CHERRY CAKE

SERVES 8–10

120g butter

120g caster sugar

3 drops vanilla extract

175g plain flour

¼ teaspoon baking powder

3 eggs, lightly beaten

250g fresh pitted cherries or
    250g glacé cherries, chopped

Dad stocked at least six different types of cherries – glacé, crystallized, maraschino, bottled, tinned and fresh – so that he could use what he felt was the most suitable type to produce the best results. He used glacé cherries in cherry cake, but I use fresh cherries. There is no right or wrong way – it depends on your cherry preference.

Preheat the oven to 180°C/gas mark 4. Line a 15cm cake tin that is about 7cm deep with baking parchment.

Cream together the butter, sugar and vanilla extract until the mixture is light and fluffy. Sift the flour and baking powder into a separate bowl.

Add about 1 tablespoon of the beaten egg to the butter-and-sugar mixture and mix it in well before adding one-quarter of the flour. Now mix in one-third of the remaining egg followed by one-third of the remaining flour. Continue in this way until all the egg and flour are incorporated.

Fold half of the cherries into the mixture, ensuring they are well distributed. Spoon the batter into the prepared cake tin. Sprinkle the remaining cherries on top.

Bake for 30 minutes, then reduce the heat to 160°C/gas mark 3 and bake for another 40 minutes or until the cake is firm to the touch and a skewer inserted into the centre comes out clean.

when Peter met Frankie

LEMON CHEESECAKE

SERVES 8-10

FOR THE BISCUIT BASE

250g digestive biscuits
100g butter, plus extra for greasing
1 teaspoon ground ginger

FOR THE FILLING

170g cream cheese
100g caster sugar
135g lemon jelly cubes
Grated zest of 1 lemon
410g can of evaporated milk

Lemon cheesecake was not on the tea shop menu, but I've included it here as this was one of Mum's favourite family recipes, dating back to the sixties. She often made this cheesecake for dinner parties at home and on special family occasions. Everyone loved this cake and the fact that Mum made the dessert.

Grease a 23cm springform cake tin.

Crush the biscuits in a food processor or put them into a plastic food bag and bash them with a rolling pin.

Melt the butter in a saucepan over a gentle heat, then mix in the crushed biscuits and ginger. Spoon the mixture into the prepared tin. Use the back of a spoon to press the biscuit mixture evenly into the tin. Place the tin in the refrigerator for about 40 minutes to allow the biscuit base to set.

Meanwhile, mix the cream cheese with the sugar and set aside.

Melt the jelly in a cup with 150ml water in a microwave on a low setting.

Add the lemon zest to the jelly. Allow the jelly to cool a little, then pour it from a height into the cream cheese mixture to allow it to cool enough before it solidifies again.

In a separate bowl, beat the evaporated milk until it is thick, then add it to the cream cheese-and-jelly mixture. Pour the mixture on top of the biscuit base. Leave it to set in the refrigerator for 3 hours or overnight. Serve each slice with fresh raspberries or strawberries and cream.

when Peter met Frankie

FRANGIPANE TART

SERVES 8–10

FOR THE PASTRY

100g plain flour, plus extra to dust

60g butter, plus extra for greasing

Approximately ½ egg (you need 20g), beaten

40g caster sugar

FOR THE FRANGIPANE FILLING

110g caster sugar

110g butter

Approximately 2–3 eggs (you need 110g), beaten

60g cake crumbs

60g plain flour

40g ground almonds

½ teaspoon almond extract

FOR THE DECORATION

3 tablespoons apricot jam

2–3 teaspoons water

100g icing sugar

This is a classic almond-infused tart that is perfect to share with a loved one. When I found some of Dad's recipe notes I came across the ingredients for 'frangipane' – there were no tart details. I wanted to share Dad's frangipane filling, with its subtle almond taste and scent that always transport me to the tea shop.

Preheat the oven to 180°C/gas mark 4. Grease a 20cm round cake tin and line the base with a circle of baking parchment.

Rub together the flour and the butter until the mixture resembles fine cake crumbs.

Add the eggs to the caster sugar and mix them together – this allows the sugar grains to dissolve into the egg so that the sugar is evenly distributed throughout the pastry. Add the egg-and-sugar mix to the flour mix, then knead them together. Wrap the dough in cling film and place in the refrigerator for 30 minutes.

Roll out the pastry on a floured surface to fit the base of the prepared cake tin. Place the pastry in the tin, then pierce it all over with a fork. Bake for 15 minutes. Allow the pastry to cool, then spread a thin layer of apricot jam over it.

Preheat the oven once again to 180°C/gas mark 4.

To make the frangipane filling, cream the sugar and butter together until the mixture is light and creamy. Gradually add the eggs. Now add the cake crumbs, flour, ground almonds and almond extract. Mix the ingredients together gently, then spoon the mixture into the tin onto the pastry base. Bake for approximately 30 minutes until golden brown.

When you remove the tart from the oven, gently heat the apricot jam in a small pan until warm or in a microwave for 1 minute until soft. Turn the tart out of the tin and brush a thin layer of warmed apricot jam over the top of the tart while it is still warm from the oven.

Add the water to the icing sugar a little at a time until the icing has the right consistency to coat the back of a spoon. Spread the icing on top of the warm apricot jam and leave this to set.

baker's tip

You can add a couple of extra drops of almond extract to give a stronger almond flavour.

STRAWBERRY TARTS

MAKES 18 TARTS *

FOR THE SWEET PASTRY

200g plain flour, plus extra to dust
125g butter, plus extra for greasing
Approximately 1 egg (you need 40g),
    beaten
1 teaspoon vanilla extract
75g caster sugar

FOR THE FILLING

400g strawberries, halved
4 tablespoons smooth apricot jam

* depending on the size of the tart tins

Strawberry tarts with fresh cream were the summer number one choice for many. Dad only made them when strawberries were in season. We often picked the strawberries ourselves from the local pick-your-own farm. Dad also made dessert fruit flans, including strawberry; the fruit fillings varied depending on what was in season.

Preheat the oven to 180°C/gas mark 4. Grease the tart tins.

Rub together the flour and butter until the mixture resembles fine cake crumbs. Add the egg and the vanilla extract to the caster sugar in another bowl and mix them together. This allows the sugar grains to dissolve into the egg so that the sugar is evenly distributed throughout the pastry. Add the egg/sugar mix to the flour mix and knead the ingredients together.

Wrap the dough in cling film and chill in the refrigerator for 30 minutes.

Roll out the pastry on a floured surface to a thickness of about 5mm. Using a round cutter, cut out circles that are slightly bigger than your tart tins and gently press these into the prepared tins.

Bake for 8–10 minutes or until the pastry cases are light golden, then allow them to cool in the tins.

Arrange the strawberry halves in the tart cases (you'll need approximately 4 medium strawberry halves to a case).

Gently heat the smooth apricot jam in a small pan until warm or in a microwave for 1 minute until soft, then brush the warm jam over the strawberries in the tart cases, ensuring all the fruit is covered in jam. Leave on a wire rack to set. Turn out the tarts from the tart tins just before serving or displaying.

baker's tip

If you like, you can finish with a swirl of whipped cream on top of each tart once the jam has set. Also, you can always switch the strawberries for a different fruit, such as raspberries, grapes or blueberries.

when Peter met Frankie

CHOCOLATE FLORENTINES

MAKES 20

25g butter

75g caster sugar

15g plain flour

4 tablespoons double cream

50g glacé cherries, chopped

100g flaked almonds

50g mixed peel

100g dark chocolate (with 70 per cent cocoa solids)

Dad made Florentines regularly for the tea shop; they were especially popular at Christmas as gifts, presented in gold boxes tied with red ribbon. He also made tiny versions as petit fours. I like to make mine in a muffin tray – it gives them a smooth, rounded edge.

Preheat the oven to 190°C/gas mark 5. Line a baking sheet or muffin tin with baking parchment.

Melt the butter and sugar in a medium saucepan, ensuring the butter melts over a low heat. Stir it constantly so it doesn't caramelize. Now stir in the flour and gradually add the cream. Bring the mixture to the boil and stir it constantly until it thickens slightly and comes away from the sides of the pan. Take the pan off the heat and stir in the cherries, almonds and mixed peel.

Place spoonfuls of the mixture onto the prepared baking sheet, shaping them into flattened circles. Alternatively, press the mixture into the bottom of the holes of a 12-hole muffin tin.

Bake for 6–8 minutes until the Florentines are lightly golden. Allow them to cool slightly on the baking sheet or in the muffin tin, then transfer them to a wire rack using a palette knife.

Melt the chocolate in a bowl set over a pan of simmering water. Remove the pan from the heat.

Carefully pick up a Florentine and, holding it around the edge, dip the smooth underside in the chocolate. Continue until all the Florentines have been dipped in this way. If you feel unconfident about dipping them, spread the melted chocolate over each Florentine with a knife. In order to achieve a more professional appearance, rather than using a smooth knife to remove excess chocolate, use a ribbed plastic scraper to drag the excess chocolate across the biscuit base, shifting the tool left to right as you go, leaving a zigzag ribbed pattern.

Leave the Florentines, chocolate-side up, on a fresh sheet of baking parchment to set.

when Peter met Frankie

FONDANT FANCIES

MAKES 16

175g soft margarine or butter

175g caster sugar

2 large eggs

175g self-raising flour

1 teaspoon vanilla extract

2 tablespoons milk

FOR THE BUTTERCREAM

110g butter

500g icing sugar

3 tablespoons milk

1 teaspoon vanilla extract

FOR THE DECORATION

2 tablespoons apricot jam

70g marzipan

500g baker's fondant or fondant icing

A selection of food colourings (I like pink, yellow and violet)

50g dark chocolate, broken into pieces (optional)

Dips, as we called fondant fancies, are petite cakes that were made in all our family tea shops. My brother Johnny helped Dad to dip the cakes and had to be careful not to burn his fingers in the fondant. They were decorated with fondant icing in different colours: pink, yellow and white. Dad often recreated dominoes with chocolate dots on these fancies. You can be as creative as time allows with the decoration. These pretty fondant fancies always brighten up afternoon tea.

Preheat the oven to 180°C/gas mark 4. Line a 20cm square tin with baking parchment.

Prepare the sponge using the method given for the lemon drizzle cake (see page 150), omitting the lemon zest and substituting vanilla extract for the lemon extract. Spoon the mixture into the prepared tin and smooth the top with a palette knife. Bake for 35 minutes or until the cake is golden brown and springy and a skewer inserted into the centre comes out clean. Leave the cake to cool in the tin for 10 minutes, then turn it out of the tin and leave it to cool on a wire rack. Once cool, wrap the sponge in baking parchment and place it in the refrigerator until it is firm. Ideally, leave it to firm for 24 hours before using. It is essential the sponge is firm.

The next day, when you are ready to decorate, gently heat the apricot jam in a small pan until warm or in a microwave for 1 minute until soft. Meanwhile, slice the top crust off the sponge, then spread the top with the warmed apricot jam.

Roll out the marzipan very thinly and place this on top of the jam layer. Using a sharp cake knife, cut the cake into 16 even rectangles that are 2.5 x 5cm and set aside.

Now prepare the buttercream. In a mixing bowl, beat together the butter, half of the icing sugar and half of the milk until the mixture is smooth. Gradually add the remaining icing sugar and milk, as well as the vanilla extract, and continue to beat the mixture until it is smooth. Brush the sides of the cakes with buttercream, set them on a tray and transfer them to the refrigerator. Leave them there to set for 2 hours or, preferably, overnight to ensure they are firm.

If you are using baker's fondant, heat the fondant in a bowl set over a pan of simmering water until it has a soft consistency and appears glossy.

Divide the icing between several bowls, depending on how many colours you are using. Mix a few drops of food colouring into each bowl of icing except for 1, which you can use to make white fancies. Plunge a fork into the base of 1 cake at an angle, dip the cake completely in a bowl of icing and immediately place the fondant-coated sponge, base-down, on a wire rack, removing the fork carefully. Repeat with the remaining cakes until they have all been dipped in icing. Leave the dips on a wire rack until the icing has set, which will take roughly an hour.

If baker's fondant is unavailable, warm the fondant icing in the microwave, then place it in a bowl with 4 tablespoons bun glaze (see page 168 for a recipe). Beat the mixture until it has a batter-like consistency. Dip each rectangle of sponge into the fondant, covering the top and sides, then place it upright on a cooling rack and leave it to set.

If you would like to add more decoration, melt the chocolate in a bowl set over a pan of simmering water. Fill a piping bag with the melted chocolate and pipe the chocolate in lines, swirls and patterns onto the fondant fancies. Enjoy decorating the cakes. You can create a domino pattern on white fancies quite easily using the melted chocolate to make dots, as Peter did. Leave the decorated fancies on a wire rack until the chocolate has set completely.

When set, remove the fancies from the wire rack using a palette knife and place each one into a cake case.

when Peter met Frankie

ENGLISH MADELEINES

100g self-raising flour
A pinch of salt
100g butter, plus extra for greasing
100g caster sugar
2 eggs

FOR THE DECORATION

3 tablespoons smooth apricot jam
50g desiccated coconut
5 glacé cherries, halved

These conical English madeleines, coated in coconut and with a cherry on top, symbolize traditional afternoon tea. The taste of the delicate sponge with the cherry and coconut always gives me 'a remembrance of things past', as French writer Marcel Proust discovered when he tasted the French madeleines served at tea by his aunt. Whenever I set eyes on a madeleine, I want to recapture the past – afternoon tea, with customers enjoying madeleines, the pretty sight and scent of the cakes, the warm atmosphere in the tea shop, Mum behind the counter and Dad in the bakehouse.

Preheat the oven to 180°C/gas mark 4. Grease 10 large dariole moulds.

Mix the flour and salt in a bowl. Cream together the butter and sugar in another bowl until the mixture is light. Beat in the eggs, then stir in the flour and salt.

Divide the mixture evenly between the moulds and bake for about 15 minutes. Leave the cakes to cool a little in the moulds, then transfer them to a wire rack to cool completely.

Trim off the ends of the cakes and spread the coconut flakes on a plate. Gently heat the jam in a small pan until warm or in a microwave for 1 minute until soft, then brush the warm jam over the top and sides of the cakes. Roll each cake in the coconut. Decorate the top of each madeleine with half a glacé cherry.

baker's tip

Add extra chopped cherries to the sponge if you like.
Pierce the base of each cake with a skewer or fork and
use this to hold the cake while rolling it in coconut.

love on a plate

chapter three

Customers as Cakes
Classic Tea Shop Cakes

Frankie became engaged to Peter and moved to Weybridge in the Spring of 1960, when she started working in the tea shop alongside Peter's mother and father, Nana and Papa, who by this time had closed their own tea shop and were helping Peter establish his business. She lived with Peter's family in Weybridge Park and worked behind the counter with Nana and also waitressed. The roles were clearly divided: women at the front serving customers, men out the back preparing the food. Mum's previous job was as an operating theatre sister at London's Orthopaedic Hospital. She swapped handling surgical instruments for cake tongs and switched patients for customers. If Dad was the soul of the tea shop, Mum was the heart.

On 10 October 1960, they married in St Charles's Catholic Church, a few hundred yards away from *Peter's*, where they held their wedding reception. Not surprisingly, Dad made the wedding cake and all the pastries. The bride and groom posed in the tea room, where they sealed their love and tea shop future.

After a two-week honeymoon in Brighton, they returned to Weybridge where they settled into tea shop life as if it was all they had ever known. Daily life mirrored the *Peter's* menu: morning coffee (from 9 a.m. until midday), light lunches (from midday to 2 p.m.) and afternoon tea (from 3 p.m. to 5 p.m.). Peter rose early every day (4.30 a.m.) and had a fixed routine: he baked bread first, followed by buns, pastries, scones, savouries and fresh cream cakes. In the afternoons he made the batch cakes and celebration cakes and he prepared customer orders. Every evening, he placed trays of meringues in the oven, the door left ajar overnight after baking for about an hour and a half, so they could cool and dry out slowly overnight. By dawn, when he arrived for work, the meringues were perfect. The classic cakes in the late fifties and sixties were Victoria sandwich, Madeira cake, seed cake, Dundee cake and Battenberg. On Saturdays, I remember Dad made a wider selection of breads and more elaborate cakes for the weekend crowd, such as croissants, brioche and millefeuille. On Mondays, when the tea shop closed, he made chocolates and speciality cakes.

Dad's routine changed during the two busiest times in the tea shop calendar, Christmas and Easter, when he worked longer hours to create all the festive food. When he had opened the tea shop on 10 December 1958, he told me that the first thing he had made was chocolate peppermints while the workmen fitted the oven. With just fifteen days to go before Christmas, he then made heaps of mince pies, Christmas biscuits and cakes, and his first Christmas at *Peter's* was a success. At Easter, Dad always made mounds of hot cross buns, simnel cake and chocolate Easter eggs and figurines. On Easter Sunday, he gave each of us our own chocolate egg with our names piped on it in white icing, decorated with pastel-coloured flowers and with little surprises inside: mini eggs, a plastic chick and some money. He made an extra large egg for Mum, intricately decorated and packed inside with personal gifts.

Frankie's daily routine involved arriving at the bakehouse entrance at 8 a.m., when she transferred the freshly made bread, buns, pastries and scones onto counter trays and placed a selection in the window and cake cabinets. Each type of cake and bun had its allotted place, with *Peter's* signature cream meringues taking prime position in the window. There was a certain art to creating window displays and, over the years, themes ranged from Remembrance Day and St George's Day to those inspired by one-off occasions such as the Queen's Silver Jubilee in 1977. On Saturdays and during holidays, I helped Mum fill the counter trays and position them in the cabinets. Mum also prepared the glass cake stands for the afternoon with eight cream cakes on a white doily, always with a meringue in the middle.

THE TEA SHOP WAS OUR HOME and it was a home with many visitors, too. Some we knew by name, others only by cake. Mrs Meringue, a well-heeled Weybridge lady, regularly bought meringues for her tea parties at her mansion on St George's Hill. "I'll have four of the biggest meringues," she said in her upper-class voice. "I'd like that one, that one, that one and that one." She pointed her manicured finger at the largest meringues on the tray. Cream meringues were hard to pick up with hands or tongs. Being a nurse, Mum had a delicate touch. She retrieved the tray of meringues from the window, placed it by the till, lifted up each one that Mrs Meringue had pointed to with the silver plated tongs and placed it in a white cake box. "No, no, not that one, that one." She leaned over the counter and pointed at the biggest meringue on the tray.

"Here you are. I hope you enjoy them." Frankie handed the box to the lady.

DESCRIPTION *SIGNALEMENT*

	Bearer *Titulaire*	★ Wife *Femme*
Profession *Profession*	CONFECTIONER, NETTLESTONE	HOUSEWIFE
Place and date of birth *Lieu et date de naissance*	RYDE, I.o.W. 29.4.1931	LONDON 23.4.1936
Country of Residence *Pays de Résidence*	ENGLAND.	ENGLAND
Height *Taille*	5 ft 10½ in.	5 ft 4½ in.
Colour of eyes *Couleur des yeux*	BROWN	BLUE
Colour of hair *Couleur des cheveux*	BROWN	BROWN
Special peculiarities *Signes particuliers*	—	

★CHILDREN *ENFANTS*

Name *Nom*	Date of birth *Date de naissance*	Sex *Sexe*

Usual signature of bearer
Signature du titulaire

Usual signature of wife
Signature de sa femme

Peter's

(WEYBRIDGE) LTD.

Telephone: Weybridge 843282

27 CHURCH STREET
WEYBRIDGE
SURREY

1 Dad described himself as a confectioner in their shared passport. 2 Mum, pretty in Paris, 1962. 3 *Peter's* pink menu, the enduring symbol of the tea shop. 4 One of my favourite images of Dad in the bakehouse, making another batch of Japonaise. 5 *Peter's* tea room around 1958, with Lloyd Loom chairs and the clock that chimed every quarter of an hour.

"Thank you so much. Afternoon tea wouldn't be the same without Peter's meringues. Not that my ladies know Peter makes them!"

The staff had their favourite tea shop classics. Everyone had a coffee or tea break, for which they were allowed to choose a cake. At Christmas time, mince pies were popular, but staff chose whatever cake they fancied. When the tea room closed from 2–3 p.m., the waitresses sat down for lunch with Mum. On Saturdays, when I waitressed, I joined the staff table. Dad always passed the food through the hatch. It was a ritual for the weekly waitresses, Kitty and Joan, to follow their main course with a triangle of piping hot homemade apple pie with cloves.

After lunch, Kitty served tea and cakes in the tea room from 3–5 p.m. The cake stands containing cream cakes took centre stage on each table.

One Indian gentleman, or Mr Victoria Sponge, always sat under the clock on his own. As soon as he walked through the door we knew his order: a pot of tea, a Welsh rarebit and a tray of cream cakes including a slice of Victoria sponge. He had a habit of arriving at five to five, just before the shop closed, and stayed until all the tables had been cleared. His wife was in India looking after her elderly parents so he craved company as much as cakes. "How are your studies? What do you want to do when you grow up?" he asked, like a kind uncle.

At the end of each day, Fuby and I helped Kitty move the ten tables and their chairs so she could hoover up all the crumbs. It was like a treasure trove as we picked up coins from under the tables. At first, I thought the customers were clumsy, leaving coins everywhere, until one day I spotted Kitty dropping them out of her pocket for her little helpers.

If there were any fresh cakes left over I put them into little boxes for the staff to take home before helping Mum count up the day's takings. I put crushed cakes in a box for our family. Years after the shop closed, former members of staff contacted me to share memories of *Peter's*. A few recalled how much they treasured those boxes of leftover cakes. I loved the crushed cakes, our end-of-day treat at home.

THERE WERE RARELY ANY MERINGUES LEFT for staff or family. Crisp on the outside and chewy inside, Peter's meringues were hard to resist. The recipe for these meringues is included in this chapter, along with many other classic tea shop cakes that proved time and again to be favourites with the customers at *Peter's* – the most popular baked goods to leave Dad's bakehouse.

BATTENBERG

SERVES 6–8

175g butter, plus extra for greasing

175g caster sugar, plus extra for sprinkling

3 large eggs, beaten

175g self-raising flour

2–3 drops red food colouring

200g raspberry jam

275g almond paste or marzipan

Although Dad regularly made traditional cakes, he enjoyed adding his own individual touch. One year, he changed the colour and pattern of the Battenberg cake from pink and yellow checks to create a St George's Cross in maroon and white. St George's Day is on Mum's birthday, April 23, so there was always a double celebration.

Preheat the oven to 160°C/gas mark 3. Grease an 18cm square cake tin and line it with baking parchment.

Cream together the butter and sugar until the mixture is light, then add the beaten eggs and, if the mixture begins to curdle, a little flour. Fold in the remaining flour. Divide the mixture into 2 and add the food colouring to one batch of batter. Stir it in well.

Place some folded baking parchment in the cake tin in the centre to keep the 2 colours separate. Spoon the pink mixture on 1 side of the baking parchment and the plain mixture the other side. Smooth the top gently using a palette knife. Bake for 30–35 minutes or until the cake is firm but springy and a skewer inserted into the centre of the cakes comes out clean. Leave the cakes to cool in the tin for 5 minutes, then turn them out onto a wire rack and leave to cool completely.

When cool, trim the sides of the cakes to give them nice, crisp straight edges. Then make a vertical cut down the centre of each cake to divide it into 2, so that you have 4 long strips, 2 of each colour.

Gently heat the raspberry jam in a small pan until warm or in a microwave for 1 minute until soft. Apply a thin layer with a brush on all sides of the pink and plain sponge strips. Place 2 sponges, 1 of each colour, on the work surface to make the base layer of the cake, then position the remaining 2 on top, ensuring a pink sponge is placed over a plain one and vice versa, as in the picture opposite.

Heat the majority of the remaining jam gently in a pan until it is warm. Using a pastry brush, coat the top, base and sides of the cake (not the ends) with a layer of warm jam.

Roll out the marzipan to the length of the cake and so that it is wide enough to cover the sides and base of the cake. Sprinkle the caster sugar on the board and rolling pin as this stops the marzipan sticking. Place the cake on the marzipan and gently fold the marzipan over the sponge. Seal the join with a little jam. Turn the cake over so that the seal is on the base. Gently smooth the cake. Trim each end of the cake neatly. Lightly mark the top with a crisscross pattern, scoring the marzipan with the back of a knife, to give the cake a professional finish.

customers as cakes

VICTORIA SPONGE

SERVES 10

225g caster sugar

225g butter, plus extra for greasing

Approximately 4 eggs (you need 225g), beaten

1 teaspoon vanilla essence

225g self-raising flour

285g raspberry or other jam, to fill

Icing sugar, to dust

FOR THE BUTTERCREAM

100g icing sugar

50g butter

2 drops vanilla extract

This sponge cake, filled with jam and cream and dusted with icing sugar, is one of the nation's favourite sponges. We sold Victoria sponge as a whole cake, but if there were any left over towards the end of the day, they would be cut up and sold as individual slices in the tea room. One day, someone ordered a Victoria sponge with lemon curd filling instead of the traditional jam-and-cream filling, which Dad made, much to his amusement.

Preheat the oven to 180ºC/gas mark 4. Grease 2 x 18cm sandwich cake tins and line them with baking parchment.

Cream the sugar and butter together until the mixture is light and fluffy. Beat in the eggs and the vanilla essence a little at a time. Gently fold in the flour.

Divide the batter equally between the prepared sandwich tins and bake for 20–25 minutes or until a skewer inserted into the centre of the cakes comes out clean. Turn out the cakes onto a wire rack to allow them to cool completely.

To make the buttercream, mix the icing sugar with the butter and beat the mixture well with a wooden spoon. Mix in the vanilla extract. Set this mixture aside, in the refrigerator if you're baking on a hot day, otherwise at room temperature – you don't want it to be too hard for spreading.

Once the cakes are cool, sandwich them together with jam and the buttercream or, alternatively, some freshly whipped cream. You can also use strawberries, raspberries or cherries to fill this cake or place on top of it. Dust icing sugar over the top of the cake.

baker's tip

To make a chocolate version of this cake, reduce the flour by 50g and replace it with 50g cocoa.

customers as cakes

MADEIRA SPONGE

SERVES 10

175g butter, plus extra for greasing

175g caster sugar

Grated zest of 1 lemon

3 eggs

2 tablespoons milk

250g plain flour

1 teaspoon baking powder

Caster sugar, for dredging

3 strips of lemon zest

Dad made Madeira sponge as a batch cake every week and it was popular with the older generation who liked to keep one in the house for unexpected guests. It is a light, golden sponge that's very satisfying with a cup of tea or glass of Madeira wine, as was the tradition. I like to picture the Weybridge ladies serving a slice of Dad's Madeira sponge and enjoying a civilized drink together.

Preheat the oven to 180°C/gas mark 4. Grease an 18cm round cake tin and line it with baking parchment.

Cream the butter and sugar with the grated lemon zest until the mixture is light and fluffy. Combine the eggs and milk in a large bowl, then slowly add the creamed mixture, beating well. Sift the flour and baking powder in a separate bowl, then fold this into the creamed mixture.

Pour the batter into the prepared cake tin and sprinkle a little caster sugar on top. Bake for 25 minutes, then place the lemon zest on top and bake for another 30 minutes.

Leave the cake in the tin to stand for 10 minutes, then turn it out onto a wire rack and leave it to cool.

baker's tip

Be quick when you open and close the oven to place the lemon zest on the cake – to avoid too much heat escaping, which spoils the baking process.

DUNDEE CAKE

SERVES 10-12

275g plain flour

½ teaspoon salt

½ teaspoon baking powder

1½ teaspoons mixed spice

225g soft brown sugar

175g butter, plus extra for greasing

50g white vegetable fat (such as Cookeen)

4 large eggs

50g ground almonds

225g sultanas

100g currants

100g raisins

100g candied peel

100g glacé cherries, rinsed, dried and quartered

Grated zest of 1 lemon

50g almond halves

FOR THE GLAZE

2 teaspoons caster sugar

1 tablespoon milk

This light fruitcake (as opposed to a rich one), stuffed with raisins, sultanas, currants and peel and decorated with sliced almonds, is a great cake to take with you on holiday as it lasts for weeks. When we went on family holidays to Dartmouth we always packed several cakes. This is Mum's variation – one slice is a mini-meal in itself and there's so much fruit in it, it must be good for you.

Preheat the oven to 160°C/gas mark 3. Grease a 20cm round cake tin that is at least 7cm deep and line it with baking parchment.

Sift the flour, salt, baking powder and mixed spice into a bowl. Set aside.

Cream together the sugar, butter and fat until the mixture is soft. Lightly whisk the eggs and add them gradually to the creamed mixture with 1 tablespoon of the flour.

Fold the ground almonds into the flour mixture, then fold the flour into the creamed mixture using a metal spoon. Add all the dried fruit, glacé cherries and grated lemon zest and mix them in well.

Spoon the batter into the prepared tin and press the centre of the cake downwards with the back of a large metal spoon. This stops the cake from peaking in the centre during cooking. Arrange the almond halves around the top of the cake.

Place the tin on a baking sheet and bake for 1 hour, then reduce the heat to 150°C/gas mark 2 and bake for a further 2 hours.

Test the cake and, when you feel it is almost cooked, prepare the glaze. Dissolve the sugar in the milk in a pan set over a low heat. Then brush the glaze onto the top of the cake while warm (with a pastry brush). Return the cake to the oven for a final 5 minutes of cooking.

customers as cakes

CARAWAY SEED CAKE

SERVES 8-10

175g caster sugar

175g butter, plus extra for greasing

200g self-raising flour

3 eggs

2 teaspoons caraway seeds

25g ground almonds

1 tablespoon milk

Aunty Mary, my Godmother and Dad's sister, gave me this seed cake recipe after she made it for me one day. I'd gone to see her and Dad's other sister, my Aunty Hazell, to share memories of the family tea shops. Dad also made seed cake but it wasn't something I ate as a child – it's an acquired, subtle taste. Now seed cake always reminds me of my lovely Aunty Mary. This cake is a good one to make for any elderly friends or neighbours as a treat – a remembrance of teatime in a bygone age.

Preheat the oven to 180°C/gas mark 4. Grease a 20cm cake tin that's 3cm deep and line it with baking parchment.

Cream sugar and butter together. Sift the flour into a separate bowl. Add the eggs, one at a time, to the creamed butter and sugar, each with 1 tablespoon of the flour. Add caraway seeds, ground almonds and the remaining flour and fold them in. Stir in the milk, being careful not to beat the mixture too harshly so as to create a light sponge.

Pour the batter into the prepared tin and level off the top with a palette knife. Bake in the centre of the oven for about 1 hour or until the cake is springy.

customers as cakes

ICED WALNUT CAKE

SERVES 10–12 SLICES

255g caster sugar

225g butter, softened, plus extra for greasing

4 eggs, beaten

250g self-raising flour

115g walnuts, roughly chopped

500g baker's fondant icing or 200g soft fondant icing, to decorate

2 tablespoons apricot jam (if using soft fondant)

8–10 walnut halves, to decorate

FOR THE BUTTERCREAM

120g icing sugar

120g butter

Mum recalls the iced walnut sponge in *Fuller's* tea room on Regent Street, where she enjoyed afternoon tea and cake on her days off from her nursing shifts. Dad made iced walnut cake every week, which, for Mum, was pure nostalgia for her nursing days. Mum tested Dad's recipe, impressing all those who saw and tasted it as she had recreated Dad's iced walnut cake perfectly.

Preheat the oven to 180°C/gas mark 4. Grease 2 x 20cm round cake tins and line them with baking parchment.

Cream the sugar and butter together until the mixture is light and fluffy. Gradually add the eggs to the mixture. Add 1 tablespoon flour if the mixture begins to curdle. Lightly fold in the remaining flour. Fold the chopped walnuts through the mixture, ensuring that they are evenly distributed.

Divide the mixture equally between the prepared tins and bake for 20–25 minutes or until a skewer inserted into the centre of the cakes comes out clean. Leave the cakes to cool in the tins for 5 minutes, then turn them out onto a wire rack to cool completely.

To make the buttercream, place the icing sugar and butter in a bowl and beat them together for 3–4 minutes until the mixture is light and fluffy. Cover the top of 1 cake with the buttercream, then place the other cake on top.

Heat the baker's fondant icing in a bowl set over a pan of simmering water. Pour the warmed fondant in a steady stream over the top and sides of the cake. Use a palette knife to smooth out the icing all over.

Alternatively, you can roll out some ready-to-roll fondant icing and smooth it over the cake. If using soft, ready-to-roll fondant icing, gently heat the apricot jam in a small pan until warm or in a microwave for 1 minute until soft. Brush warmed apricot jam over the cake surface – this helps the fondant to stick. (However, you don't need jam for baker's fondant as this sticks naturally.)

Decorate the top of the cake with the halved walnuts. If you're using baker's fondant, leave the icing to set for about 15 minutes. (Ready-to-roll fondant doesn't need to set.)

CREAM MERINGUES

MAKES 12-14 HALVES, 6-7 MERINGUES

150ml egg whites
350g caster sugar

FOR THE FILLING

275ml double cream
1 tablespoon caster sugar

Former customers mourned the loss of Peter's meringues probably more than any other cake when the tea shop closed in 2000. I've given some of Dad's tips here to help you make your own. He always left his meringues in the oven overnight with the oven door slightly open, he was scrupulous about sterilizing equipment and he sandwiched the meringues together with fresh cream whipped with some caster sugar.

Preheat the oven to 110°C/gas mark ¼. Line a baking sheet with some baking parchment.

First, sterilize your mixing bowl. Carefully pour boiling water from a kettle into it, then empty it out and ensure it is completely dry.

Using either a whisk, electric whisk or freestanding food mixer, beat the egg whites until stiff. Gradually add half the sugar and mix; you should achieve a glossy finish with stiff peaks. Gently tip the remaining sugar into the bowl and fold it in. Peter used the age old trick of ensuring the mixture doesn't fall out of the bowl when held upside down over your head to know when it was stiff enough.

Spoon the mixture into a piping bag fitted with a 1cm nozzle, then pipe 12–14 shells that are roughly the size of half a tennis ball onto the prepared baking sheet. (To fix the baking parchment to the tray, dab a few splodges of meringue mixture onto the tray and stick the paper down using these.) There will be minimal expansion, so space the meringue shells about 2cm apart.

Bake for 2 hours, then turn off the oven and leave the meringues in there overnight with the door slightly open.

Whip up the fresh cream, adding the sugar. Pipe the cream onto a meringue half and sandwich this together with another half.

The meringues can be stored in an airtight container for up to a week.

baker's tip

If you don't want to sandwich meringues together with cream, you can always make individual meringue nests which you can fill with fruit and cream to make mini-pavlovas. If you wish to flavour your meringues, try adding 2 teaspoons cocoa to the caster sugar in the filling and fold it in just a few times so that you are left with a marbled effect. To change the colour of the meringues, add a few drops of food colouring to the meringue mixture. These are always popular with children, and are great for birthday parties.

customers as cakes

CHRISTMAS CAKE

SERVES 10–12

275g sultanas

400g raisins

150g currants

110g mixed peel

200g glacé cherries, chopped

Grated zest of 1 lemon

Grated zest of 1 orange

Juice of ½ lemon

250ml brandy or sherry

175g butter, softened, plus extra for greasing

175g dark muscovado sugar

25g black treacle

3 eggs, beaten

220g plain flour

25g glycerine

1 teaspoon mixed spice

1 teaspoon cinnamon

40g ground almonds

FOR THE DECORATION

2 tablespoons apricot jam

Caster sugar, to sprinkle

800g marzipan or almond paste (see page 96)

800g royal icing

baker's tip

If someone likes rich fruitcake, you can use this recipe as a birthday cake with candles instead of Christmas decorations.

When Dad lifted a tray of ten freshly baked Christmas cakes out of the oven, Christmas filled the bakehouse. We decorated the tea house with festive paper decorations and sold boxes of fancy crackers. Dad decorated the cakes with royal icing and created artificial rocks made out of icing sugar and water to create a pretty snow scene. Each cake had a cast of little plastic characters: a robin, a reindeer, a snowman and Father Christmas on skis.

I recommend you start preparing your Christmas cake roughly 4–5 weeks before Christmas.

Put the dried fruit and mixed peel, the glacé cherries, the lemon and orange zest, the lemon juice and 100ml of the sherry or brandy in a large bowl. Stir well, cover the bowl with cling film and set aside for 2–3 days, stirring each day.

Preheat the oven to 140ºC/gas mark 1. Grease a 20cm round cake tin that is at least 7cm deep and line it with baking parchment.

Place the butter, sugar and treacle in a bowl and beat the ingredients together until the mixture is light. Gradually add eggs to the mixture and add a little flour if it starts to curdle. Add the glycerine and sift the flour and spices over the mixture. Add the ground almonds, then fold in the soaked fruit.

Pour the batter into the prepared tin and level it off with the back of a spoon, creating a small hollow in the centre to prevent it from rising up into a peak during cooking. Bake for approximately 2 hours or until the cake is baked through. You may need to cover the top with baking parchment after about 1 hour to prevent burning the top.

Leave the cake to cool in the tin. When it is completely cool, prick the top of the cake with a skewer 8–10 times. Pour 2–3 tablespoons of brandy or sherry over the top and allow it to soak through. Wrap the cake in baking parchment or kitchen foil and store it in a cool place. Continue to add 1 tablespoon of sherry or brandy once a week until Christmas. Then the cake will be ready for icing.

Cover the cake with a layer of marzipan and icing. To do this, gently heat the apricot jam in a small pan until warm or in a microwave for 1 minute until soft. Brush the warm jam over the top and sides of the cake. Next, sprinkle caster sugar over the rolling pin and work surface. Roll out the marzipan and cover the top and sides of the cake. Place the ready-to-roll icing over the top of the marzipan icing. Neaten all the edges and place the cake on a silver cake board, if you have one. You may want to decorate your finished cake with miniature Christmas figurines, as Peter did.

customers as cakes

MINCE PIES

MAKES ABOUT 18 PASTRY CASES

FOR THE MINCEMEAT *

450g Bramley apples, peeled, chopped into chunks or finely grated

110g blanched almonds, finely chopped

110g mixed peel, finely chopped

450g seedless raisins, finely chopped

450g currants, finely chopped

450g sultanas, finely chopped

175g suet

Grated zest and juice of 1 orange

Grated zest and juice of 1 lemon

450g dark brown sugar

½ teaspoon salt

½ teaspoon cinnamon

½ teaspoon ground ginger

½ teaspoon allspice

¼ teaspoon ground nutmeg

175ml brandy

FOR THE PASTRY

230g plain flour, plus extra to dust

125g butter, plus extra for greasing

Approximately 1 egg (you need 40g), beaten

75g caster sugar, plus extra for sprinkling

* makes 8–10 x 450g jars of mincemeat, each enough for approximately 12–14 tarts

Dad made individual mince pies with shortcrust pastry or puff pastry only at Christmas time. He couldn't make them quickly enough and they were often sold straight from the oven trays. He also made large mincemeat and apples pies, which he cut and served in the tea room or sold as family pies. Sometimes he made them as open-topped shallow filled tarts with a pastry lattice on top. His recipe makes a large quantity of mincemeat, so you can give away some jars as Christmas gifts and keep the rest for making enough mince pies to take you through the entire holiday period. I've given instructions for individual shortcrust pastry pies, but you can use the filling, as Peter did, in a variety of ways.

Mix the apples, almonds, peel and fruit together in a large bowl. Add all the remaining ingredients except half of the brandy and stir everything together well. Cover the bowl with cling film and set it aside for 3 days, stirring occasionally.

After the fruit has had 3 days of soaking, add the remaining brandy and stir the mixture well. Then pack it into sterilized jars. Set the mincemeat aside for at least 2 weeks before using it to make mince pies.

When you're ready to make the mince pies, preheat the oven to 180°C/gas mark 4. Grease your tart tins (you can use jam tart tins). Rub together the flour and butter until the mixture resembles fine cake crumbs.

Add the egg to the caster sugar, then mix them together – this allows the sugar grains to dissolve into the egg so that the sugar is evenly distributed throughout the pastry. Add the egg-and-sugar mix to the flour mixture and knead them together to form a dough. Wrap the dough in cling film and chill in the refrigerator for 30 minutes.

Roll out the dough on a floured surface to a thickness of about 5mm. Using a round cutter with a circumference that is slightly larger than that of the holes in your tart tins, cut out 18 circles. Gently press these into the prepared tins. Using a slightly smaller round cutter, cut out 18 lids from the remaining dough.

Place a generous teaspoon of mincemeat in each pastry case. Brush the edges of the smaller pastry cases with egg wash and place the lid on top, gently pushing it down onto the filling to seal. Do not overfill the cases with mincemeat as it will spill out during baking and spoil the look of the pies. Brush the tops with egg wash. Bake for 15–20 minutes or until the mince pies are golden brown. Sprinkle with sugar as soon as you remove the tarts from the oven.

CHRISTMAS BISCUITS

MAKES 18–35 *

200g butter

200g caster sugar

2 eggs (or 1 egg, 1 yolk – you need 75g), beaten

400g plain flour

1 teaspoon baking powder

Pinch of salt

* depending on shape and size of the cutters

The baker's son, Johnny, always helped Dad to make the range of Christmas biscuits in the bakehouse during the last week of November and, every year, he would take one week's annual leave from the police force the week before Christmas to help Dad with all the festive orders. Dad made the biscuit bases while Johnny decorated the various shapes – Father Christmas faces, stockings, holly leaves, Christmas trees, robins and angels. Use your favourite Christmas cutters for these biscuits, which make nice gifts when arranged in cellophane bags tied with ribbon.

Preheat the oven to 180°C/gas mark 4. Line a couple of baking sheets with baking parchment.

Cream the butter and sugar together until the mixture is light and fluffy. Add the eggs, then stir in the flour, baking powder and salt. Gently but thoroughly mix the ingredients to form a dough. Wrap the dough in cling film and chill in the refrigerator for 30 minutes.

Roll out the dough to a thickness of 7mm. Using your Christmas-themed cutters, cut out your shapes. Reroll and cut the trimmings. Transfer the shapes onto the prepared baking sheets and bake for 10–12 minutes until the biscuits are light brown. Transfer them to a wire rack and leave them there to cool.

Decorate as you like with molten chocolate or icing. Opposite are 2 methods for decorating Christmas stockings and trees, based on Johnny's festive biscuits made for the shop.

customers as cakes

HOW TO DECORATE A CHRISTMAS TREE

TO DECORATE 12 BISCUITS

150g green fondant icing

3 tablespoons apricot jam

200g dark chocolate containing 70 per
cent cocoa solids

50g red royal icing (or other colour of
your choice)

Using the biscuit dough recipe on the opposite page, cut the dough using a biscuit cutter in the shape of a Christmas tree, then bake the dough as instructed opposite. Follow the instructions below to decorate the tree-shaped biscuits.

Use dark green soft, ready-to-roll fondant icing. Roll out the icing, then use a textured rolling pin to create indentations in vertical stripes that resemble the look of corduroy. Alternatively, simply leave the icing untextured. Use the Christmas tree-shaped biscuit cutter to cut the icing in the shape of the Christmas tree.

Brush heated apricot jam over the uncoated part of each biscuit, then place one foliage-shaped piece of icing on top.

Dip the trunk of each tree-shaped biscuit fully into melted chocolate. Now dip the base and sides into the melted chocolate. Place the biscuits, chocolate-side down, on a sheet of baking parchment and leave the chocolate to cool and set.

Once the chocolate has cooled and set, peel back the baking parchment.

Pipe fine balls of icing in any colour at the end of each branch to give the appearance of coloured baubles.

HOW TO DECORATE A CHRISTMAS STOCKING

TO DECORATE 12 BISCUITS

150g red fondant icing

50g white fondant icing

75g white royal icing

Using the biscuit dough recipe on the opposite page, cut the dough using a biscuit cutter in the shape of a Christmas stocking, then bake the dough as instructed opposite. Follow the instructions below to decorate the stocking-shaped biscuits.

Use soft, ready-to-roll red fondant icing. Roll it out, ideally using a textured rolling pin to create indentations in vertical stripes. Use the Christmas stocking-shaped cutter to cut the icing into stocking shapes.

Cut out a small section of white ready-to-roll icing (to resemble the white fringe of a boot) and, using a little water, stick this to the top of the stocking. Pipe a fine criss-cross pattern in white icing vertically down the centre of the stocking to simulate white laces.

Pipe a single ball of white icing onto the toe of the stocking as a bobble (similar to that found at the top of a bobble hat).

chapter four

Sweet Delights
Iconic Cakes and Tarts

Friends loved coming to tea and to birthday parties held in the tea room. Some friends even became Saturday Girls working in the tea shop with me, when we were old enough. Chocolate cream slices were, without a doubt, one of the main advantages of working on Saturdays. The other benefit was the Saturday Boys. These local Weybridge lads carried out jobs for Peter: packing cakes fresh from the oven onto counter trays, squeezing jam into doughnuts and rolling filled ones in sugar, cleaning work surfaces and floors and running errands. Aside from assisting Peter, they helped the time to pass more quickly with their cheeky banter and attempts to chat up us Saturday Girls over trays of cream cakes.

I started washing up at the age of eleven and progressed to waitressing and being a member of the counter staff. My friend, Karen, started washing up at the same time as me and began working behind the counter when she was twelve. On her first day, she stood there in her blue checked apron eagerly awaiting a customer.

In walked Mrs Millefeuille, wearing a long, flowing fur coat, who scanned the cakes and desserts in the front window and fridge as if she was a Michelin inspector. "Can I help you?" Karen asked under Frankie's guidance.

"I'd like that millefeuille." She looked down her nose at the lemon-and-cream confection, decorated with chocolate and named after the thousand leaves of pastry. Karen reached into the window to pick up the cream dessert that was popular with Weybridge ladies keen to impress guests at dinner parties. She placed it in a white cake box, cut a piece of red ribbon, wrapped it around the box and then tied it in a small bow. With a big smile, Karen handed the box to the lady. The millefeuille fell out of the bottom and slid down the woman's coat, leaving a trail of cream and lemon icing on the fur. Karen gasped while Frankie grabbed a cloth and rushed around to the ashen-faced woman.

"It's her first day." Frankie dabbed the cloth on the coat.

"What about my coat and the cake?" the woman snapped.

"We can arrange for it to be dry cleaned," Frankie said.

"I'm not worried about my coat. But I simply must have a millefeuille for my dinner party tonight."

"Of course," Frankie remained calm. "I'll get you another one on the house."

Frankie saw Karen was upset and whispered to her to go out the back, where she told Dad what had happened. He pulled out a flour tin for her to sit on and gave her a mug of tea and a chunk of chocolate sponge leftover from a chocolate fort birthday cake he had just made.

"Don't worry, dear," he said. "It's not worth getting upset over a cake."

Karen put the Mrs Millefeuille incident behind her and progressed to being a waitress on Saturdays, when regular customers came into the café for their 'morning coffee, light lunch or afternoon tea'. Like all the other waitresses, Karen wore a smart uniform of a black skirt, on the knee, with a white blouse, a welcome change from the blue checked apron worn by counter staff. Every Saturday morning at 11 a.m. a devoted retired couple, Mr and Mrs Gravelle, took their usual seats at a table for two in the alcove near the powder room. Mrs Gravelle usually enjoyed a cream meringue while Mr Gravelle was partial to a fresh cream palmier, otherwise known as elephant ears, a heart-shaped cake made of puff pastry filled with fresh cream and jam. If there were no palmiers left Peter made one fresh for Mr Gravelle by piping cream in between two pastry hearts (stored in the bakehouse) with a dollop of jam.

After coffee and cakes Mrs Gravelle always bought a gold box of Peter's rose-and-violet chocolates and a selection of petit fours. When Mr Gravelle became ill and housebound, Frankie regularly popped over to his house with cream palmiers. After he died his wife came into the shop to thank Frankie for her special home deliveries.

Mr Gravelle wasn't the only sick customer who Frankie helped. There were several wheelchair-bound customers who relied on her practical and emotional support in a tea room that, to the sick, became a cosy haven.

Whenever Mr Buckling appeared in his wheelchair at the door with his daughter, the call went out for Mrs Peters, as some customers called Frankie. Mr Buckling had run *Buckling's Bakery* on Church Street. Having retired, he enjoyed Peter's expertly made pastries and trusted only Frankie to push his wheelchair into the café without smashing into the cake cabinets. Frankie reserved him the table nearest the entrance and ordered his lunch; there were homemade Specials of the Day, which varied – cottage pie was his favourite. After a big lunch and cakes, his daughter knew there was no need for a hot meal later on.

1 Nana, proud of the family tea shop, took her role seriously.
2 Saturday Boys, Johnny and 'Wingnut': judging by the messy
aprons you can tell who did more work. 3 Smart Saturday Girls,
sporting spotless white blouses, front of house. 4 Dad and
'Stewpot' larking about in the kitchen. 5 A display of iconic
gateaux and large coffee Japonaise.

FOR MANY CUSTOMERS, a trip to *Peter's* was far more than just about consuming cakes; it was a lifeline. A young, blonde, blind girl was a regular who originally came in on her own holding a white stick. She stood at the counter talking to Mum and then sat in the café, where she relaxed amid the gentle hum of conversation, chink of china and the familiar sound of Frankie's voice. The sounds, scents and taste of homemade cakes must have been heightened for her. When she started dating a blind man, he joined her for afternoon tea in the café along with his guide dog. Frankie only allowed favoured customers to bring their dogs into the tea room, if they were well behaved and didn't bark. One eccentric lady always ordered an omelette for her dog, who sat beside her in a wicker basket on a chair.

Father Peter, the former headmaster of St George's College, regularly came into the tea shop, where he held unofficial chaplaincy meetings with parents worried about their children. Frankie introduced the customers to Father Peter, who gave his advice over a pot of tea and a toasted teacake. Father was a friend of the family who had blessed the bakehouse before it opened and, over the years, he blessed the tea room with his gentle presence. Although I didn't know it at the time, I now realize Frankie and Father Peter were 'mates' (Frankie's word) because they had several things in common: they were good listeners, they provided nourishment (for the body and soul), they were connected to St George's and they enjoyed the simple pleasure of sharing a pot of tea, cakes and conversation.

FATHER PETER was more of a homely teacake type than a millefeuille man. You'll find recipes for both of these dishes, and those for other special and iconic cakes, in this chapter.

iconic cakes and tarts

LEMON MILLEFEUILLE

SERVES 8–10

500g puff pastry (see page 132 or use shop-bought)

110g fondant icing sugar (made into fondant icing as per the packet instructions)

Juice of ½ lemon

3–4 drops yellow food colouring

55g dark chocolate, broken into pieces

250ml double cream, whipped to stiff peaks

FOR THE LEMON CURD ✳

Grated zest and juice of 3 lemons

3 eggs, beaten

225g caster sugar

60g butter

✳ *makes approximately 4 x 220g jars*

baker's tip

If you're set on making millefeuille for a particular occasion, but you're not sure if everyone is a fan of the flavour of lemon, don't worry – you can still enjoy this gorgeous dish by using plain white icing and strawberry jam in place of lemon icing and lemon curd.

When I was asked to identify which cake is the hardest one to make, I thought millefeuille would be the one. First, you have puff pastry, then two different types of icing – chocolate and lemon. The hardest part is piping the intricate chocolate pattern on top before the lemon icing sets within a matter of seconds. Dad always made it look so easy. But if I can make it, anyone can.

First make the lemon curd. Put the lemon zest and juice into a bowl set over a saucepan of simmering water with the beaten eggs, sugar and butter. Stir constantly until the mixture is nearly boiling, then remove the pan from the heat. You can use the curd once it has cooled down. It will keep in the refrigerator for 1 week.

Preheat the oven to 180ºC/gas mark 4.

Make the puff pastry following the instructions on page 132. You'll need only half of the quantity of puff pastry you make, so freeze the remaining half for a future cake. Alternatively, use shop-bought puff pastry. Roll out the puff pastry to the thickness of a one-pound coin and cut into 2 x 20cm circles. Perforate the pastry all over (to allow the air to escape during cooking) using a fork. Bake for 10–15 minutes or until the pastry is golden and crisp. Leave the pastry circles to cool on a wire rack. As the pastry circles cool from the oven, use your hand to gently flatten them by pressing down on them in order to remove any excess air.

When the pastry circles are cold, turn one of them over and place it on a chopping board. Once again, gently press down on the pastry circle with your hand to ensure a smooth, flat surface.

Mix the fondant and lemon juice together with the yellow food colouring until the mixture has a thick but pourable consistency.

Melt the chocolate in a bowl set over a saucepan of simmering water, then place it in a piping bag fitted with a fine nozzle.

Carefully pour lemon icing onto the upturned pastry circle on the chopping board. Gently spread it across the pastry with a palette knife to create a smooth and consistent surface. Before it sets, draw a spiral with the melted chocolate, working from the centre outwards across the surface of the base. Using the non-brush end of a small children's paint brush, as Peter did, create several drag marks across the surface, working from the centre to the rim, pulling the chocolate rings outwards at points to make a spider's web effect. Peter would make 8 equidistant drag marks radiating from the centre. Leave the pastry on the chopping board to allow the fondant and chocolate icing to set.

sweet delights

Carefully, use a serrated knife to trim the outer edge of the disc in order to create a perfect circle. Then cut into 8 triangular sections, ensuring each has a drag mark running across the centre. Or you could leave this top layer uncut for an alternative presentation.

Spread a generous layer of lemon curd across the other pastry circle. You'll need 2–3 tablespoons of curd, so keep the rest for other lemon curd treats. Now pipe or spread a thick layer (about 2.5cm deep) of fresh whipped cream over the entire base over the lemon curd, making this layer slightly deeper towards the centre.

If you cut the top layer of iced pastry, take the cut triangles and carefully place them on top of the cream. Peter used to push the outer edge of the triangles gently into the cream so that the triangle portions would create a roof-like effect. If you haven't cut the top layer, place it gently on top of the cream, aligning it with the base layer.

sweet delights

LEMON MERINGUE PIE

SERVES 8–10

FOR THE PASTRY BASE

100g plain flour, plus extra to dust

60g butter

20g eggs

40g caster sugar

1–2 tablespoons cold water

FOR THE FILLING

100g caster sugar

145g water

2 tablespoons cornflour

Grated zest and juice of 2 lemons

3 egg yolks

FOR THE MERINGUE

3 egg whites

100g caster sugar

This lemon meringue pie is legendary. It was served either as individual slices or sold as a whole 'pie' for Weybridge ladies keen to impress. Dad used his homemade lemon curd filling and always created a fluffy meringue topping. The lemon meringue pie may have gone in and out of fashion over the years, but it was always a classic in *Peter's*.

Preheat the oven to 180°C/gas mark 4.

To make the pastry, sift the flour into a bowl, then rub in the butter until the mixture resembles fine breadcrumbs. Add the eggs and sugar. Mix in just enough cold water for the mixture to form a stiff dough. Press the dough together lightly. Wrap the dough in cling film and rest in the refrigerator for 30 minutes.

Roll out the pastry on a floured surface, then line an 18cm pie tin with it. Pierce the dough all over, then bake it for 15 minutes.

Meanwhile, make the filling. Mix the caster sugar, the water, the cornflour, and the lemon juice and zest in a saucepan. Bring the mixture to the boil, whisking constantly, until the mixture thickens. Take the pan off the heat and leave the mixture to cool for 5 minutes, then add the egg yolks, beating well. Replace the pan over the heat and continuously whisk the mixture for 3 minutes. Then, once the pastry case is cool, spoon the filling into it.

Now make the meringue topping. In a sterilized bowl, whisk the egg whites until they form soft peaks. Add half the caster sugar and whisk until the egg whites form firm peaks, then fold in the remaining sugar. Spoon or pipe the meringue mixture on top of the lemon filling. Bake for 15–20 minutes or until the meringue is crisp. Allow to cool completely.

baker's tip

Try not to be tempted to flatten the meringue.
It looks much better when it has some volume.

PALMIERS

MAKES 11

6 tablespoons granulated sugar

25 x 30cm sheet of puff pastry
(see page 132 or use shop-bought)

250ml whipping cream

10 tablespoons jam (Dad used plum
jam traditionally but pastry chefs
often use seedless strawberry jam)

Vegetable oil, for greasing

**The big question when it comes to palmiers is – how do you eat one?
If you are brave and bite into the two pastry hearts, the cream filling
oozes out of the sides. Johnny liked to stand his palmier upright on the
plate and cut straight down the middle, chopping the heart in half.
The small pastry knives and forks we provided were perfect for this.**

Preheat the oven to 200°C/gas mark 6. Lightly grease a baking sheet
with vegetable oil.

Sprinkle some granulated sugar on your work surface. Roll out the
pastry on the sugared surface to the depth of a one-pound coin, creating
a rectangle that is 30 x 25cm. Sprinkle with some sugar and press down
with your hands. Take the right hand shorter edge of the pastry and roll
it in to the centre. Roll the left side to meet it at the centre. Brush a little
water over the pastry (using a pastry brush), then fold 1 side over the
centre and lay it on top of the other. You will now have a strip of 4 pastry
layers measuring 25 x 7cm. Straighten 1 of the short edges with a clean
cut. Now, working along the length of the pastry, cut the strip into fingers
that are about 1cm thick. Dip each finger into the sugar, then place it on
the prepared baking sheet, sugar-side down. As they bake, the palmiers
will expand outwards, but not vertically, so allow approximately 8cm
between each one.

Bake for 10–15 minutes. The pastry should be light golden and the sugar
should have caramelized. Turn each finger over on the hot baking sheet
so the sugar on the other side will slightly caramelize, but don't return
them to the oven. Allow them to cool on the tray.

Whip the cream until it is stiff.

Once the pastries are cool, gently remove them from the baking sheet
and spread jam on the least caramelized sides of half of the pastries.
Pipe whipped cream over the jam to a depth of about 2cm, as shown in
the final picture, opposite, then place the remaining pastries on top with
the caramelized sides showing.

baker's tip

You won't get an attractive, tasty, crispy side with
silicone sheeting or a non-stick sheet. Use a traditional
baking sheet with a little vegetable oil to grease it. On
the Continent, palmiers are served alone as a fancy
biscuit, which is a good use for any unfilled biscuits.

COCONUT MACAROONS

MAKES 15

Large sheet of rice paper

2 egg whites

150g caster sugar

150g desiccated coconut

1 teaspoon cornflour

50g dark chocolate (optional), broken
    into pieces

These English macaroons were always on sale in the tea shop. At first, I thought they might be too old fashioned to include in this book, but when I bit into one I loved the pure coconut taste, as well as the fact that they are crunchy on the outside, yet moist and chewy inside. I like them plain, but you can always dip them in melted chocolate, as Peter sometimes did.

Preheat the oven to 160°C/gas mark 3. Place the sheet of rice paper on a baking sheet.

Whisk the egg whites until stiff peaks form. Mix the sugar, coconut and cornflour in a bowl. Gently fold in the egg whites.

Using a dessertspoon to measure each portion, place about 15 portions of the mixture onto the rice paper and use a spoon to shape them into pyramids. Bake for about 25 minutes. They should be white after baking, so don't wait for them to go golden brown. Once they are cooked, transfer the macaroons to a wire rack and allow to cool completely.

Melt the chocolate, if using, in a bowl set over a pan of simmering water. Drizzle the chocolate over the macaroons using a spoon or a spatula.

sweet delights

CHOCOLATE CREAM SLICES

MAKES 8-10

500g puff pastry (see page 132 or use shop-bought)
100g dark chocolate, broken into pieces
240ml whipping cream
90g plum jam

My first paid job was as a washer up at the age of eleven. I was paid fifty pence an hour, which I spent on *Jackie* magazine and saved up for flares. I watched Dad make chocolate cream slices on a Saturday morning. The highlight was the bowl of leftover baked pastry smeared with chocolate, jam and whipped cream that was shared among the Saturday staff. The piping bags and mustard pots were a devil to clean, but those chocolate cream slices kept everyone happy.

Preheat oven to 180°C/gas mark 4. Line a baking sheet with baking parchment.

Roll out the puff pastry and cut it into 3 strips that are approximately 10 x 30cm. Prick the pastry all over with a fork, then place the 3 strips on the prepared baking sheet. Bake for 20–30 minutes until the pastry is golden, then transfer to a wire rack and allow them to cool.

Melt the chocolate in a bowl set over a pan of simmering water. Turn over 1 of the slices of pastry so that the smooth side is facing upwards. Cover this side with a layer of melted chocolate, spreading it evenly with a palette knife. Leave the coated strip on a wire rack to cool and allow the chocolate to set.

Whip the cream until it is stiff.

Once the chocolate has set, trim the edges and ends of the chocolate-coated pastry strip to give it straight edges and remove any areas that are not covered with chocolate. Cut across the chocolate strip to divide it into 8–10 slices.

Spread a layer of jam on the uneven (top) side of 1 pastry slice and place the next pastry slice on top of the jam. Cover the second slice with a generous layer of whipped cream that is at least 1.5cm deep.

Gently place the cut strips of chocolate-coated pastry side by side on top of the whipped cream layer, pushing them gently into place. Taking a large knife, cut down between the chocolate-coated tops through the cream, pastry and jam layers in order to form individual cream slices.

baker's tip
To ensure a clean cut, keep a large serrated knife sitting in a jug of boiling water, which you can remove and dry before each cut. The hot knife slices through chocolate without creating a mess.

BLACK FOREST GATEAU

SERVES 8-10

50g chocolate, broken into pieces
225g butter, plus extra for greasing
4 large eggs
150g caster sugar
100g plain flour
15g cocoa
1 teaspoon baking powder
5–6 tablespoons Kirsch

FOR THE FILLING AND DECORATION

410g can black cherries in syrup, stoned
300ml whipping cream
1 teaspoon caster sugar
100g chocolate vermicelli

This was one of the iconic cakes of my childhood. My friend, Karen, had the cake for her birthday for many years with 'Happy Birthday Kanga' inscribed on a chocolate disc placed on top. The combination of a light chocolate sponge infused with Kirsch, cream and cherry pie filling brings Karen's childhood birthday parties back; dancing in flares and cheesecloth shirts to Abba's 'Money, Money, Money' as her father, Keith, threw coins and notes in the air.

Preheat the oven to 180ºC/gas mark 4. Grease 2 x 20cm round cake tins and line them with baking parchment.

Melt the chocolate in a bowl set over a pan of simmering water.

Put the butter, eggs and sugar in a large bowl and whisk the ingredients together until the mixture is light and creamy. Sift the flour, cocoa and baking powder twice into another bowl, then fold the flour mixture into the egg mixture. Blend in the melted chocolate.

Divide the mixture evenly between the 2 prepared tins. Bake for approximately 35 minutes. Leave the sponges to cool in tins for 5 minutes, then tip them out onto a wire rack. When the sponges are cool, sprinkle half the Kirsch onto the sponges.

Now prepare the filling. Mix the remaining Kirsch into the cherries. Whip the cream until it is thick, then mix in the caster sugar.

Place about half of the whipped cream in a piping bag fitted with a large nozzle. Place 1 cake onto a cake board or plate and pipe a line of cream around the edge of the cake. Fill the area inside this line with half the cherries. Place the second sponge on top. Now cover the sides of the gateau with cream – use a palette knife to do this. Next, give this layer of cream a good coating of chocolate vermicelli. Pipe cream in large shells around the top edge of the gateau and fill the area inside this row of shells with the remaining cherries.

baker's tip
You can marinate 410g bottled cherries in
350ml cherry brandy to replace canned
cherries, if you fancy an alcohol-infused cake.

BAKEWELL TART

SERVES 8

115g shortcrust pastry (see page 133)

3 tablespoons smooth (seedless) raspberry jam

100g butter

100g caster sugar

2 eggs (you need 100g), beaten

2–3 drops almond extract

50g plain flour

½ teaspoon baking powder

75g ground almonds

1 tablespoon milk

FOR THE GLAZE

1 tablespoon milk

2 teaspoons caster sugar

This classic tart consists of sweet pastry, a layer of jam and a sponge centre with almonds – it is not to be confused with a Bakewell pudding or individual Bakewell cakes. If you like, you can coat the Bakewell tart with a very thin layer of icing glaze that allows you to see the tart and pretty lattice work beneath.

Separate one-third of the pastry and reserve this for the lattice work. Wrap in cling film and chill in the refrigerator.

Roll out the remaining pastry so that it is a little larger than the flan tin. Line an 18cm tart tin with the pastry, then prick the base all over with a fork. Spread the dough with a light covering of raspberry jam. Cover with cling film and place in the refrigerator for 30 minutes. Preheat the oven to 180°C/gas mark 4.

Prepare the filling. Cream the butter and sugar together until the mixture is light. Gradually add the beaten egg and almond extract, beating thoroughly as you go. Sift flour and baking powder into a bowl. Add the ground almonds. Add half of the flour-and-almond mixture to the creamed mixture and blend it in. Now mix in the remaining half, adding the milk, if needed, to soften the mixture.

Roll out the reserved pastry and cut it into 4 strips that are 2cm longer than the diameter of the flan tin. Put the mixture into the flan tin over the layer of jam and spread it to fill the pastry case. Now decorate the top of the mixture with the pastry strips in a criss-cross pattern, leaving the ends of the strips to overhang the edge of the tart tin prior to trimming them off neatly. Place the tart in the centre of the oven. Bake for between 30–40 minutes until the filling has risen and is firm.

Mix the milk and sugar together to form a glaze. Brush this over the top of the tart, covering both the pastry and the filling, then return the tart to the switched-off oven for 5 minutes. Serve warm with clotted cream or ice cream.

TEACAKES

MAKES 8

10g fast action dried yeast or 20g fresh yeast

40g caster sugar

1 teaspoon milk

150ml warm water

300g strong bread flour, plus extra for dusting

1 teaspoon salt

40g butter, softened

Approximately 1 egg (you need 25g), beaten

100g mixed dried fruit (Peter used 20 per cent mixed peel, 50 per cent sultanas, 30 per cent currants)

Vegetable oil, for greasing

FOR THE GLAZE

225g granulated sugar

3–4 tablespoons water

Dad's toasted teacakes were classic comfort food. He toasted them under a large gas grill and then slathered them with butter. The sweet scent of the teacakes wafted through to the tea room, so if customers didn't know what to order, they soon made up their mind. Dad never lost his cool as the orders for teacakes stacked up. He toasted teacakes effortlessly, despite the pressures of so many various orders, often juggling, for example, teacakes with Welsh rarebits and fruit pies with piped cream. If ever I stood in to help in the kitchen I realized you had to be on the ball, calm and skillful.

Line a baking sheet with baking parchment.

Make the dough following the instructions in the recipe for Swiss buns (see page 33). Add the fruit to the dry ingredients and mix together until they are combined and you have a soft dough. Turn out the dough onto a lightly floured surface and knead for about 10 minutes until it is smooth and elastic. Place it into a lightly oiled bowl, cover the bowl with oiled cling film and leave the bowl in a warm place for about 1½–2 hours or until the dough has doubled in size.

Turn out the risen dough onto a lightly floured surface and knock it back. Then divide it into 8 equal pieces and shape these into balls. Gently roll the balls into discs with a diameter of 9cm. Place these on the prepared baking sheet, spacing them about 3cm apart. Leave the baking sheet, uncovered, in a warm place to prove for about 30–40 minutes.

Preheat the oven to 190°C/gas mark 5. Bake for about 15 minutes or until the teacakes are golden brown and firm to the touch. Cool the teacakes on a wire rack.

To prepare the bun glaze, dissolve the granulated sugar in the water in a saucepan. Bring the mixture to the boil and boil until the liquid starts to thicken. Using a pastry brush, brush the warm glaze over all of the cooled teacakes to give them a shiny appearance. Leave the teacakes to stand for about 15 minutes, to allow the glaze to set, before serving.

baker's tip

If you have any teacakes left over the day after baking, they are best toasted and served with a generous dollop of butter.

SIMNEL CAKE

SERVES 10-12

175g caster sugar

175g butter, plus extra for greasing

3 eggs

225g plain flour

½ teaspoon grated nutmeg

½ teaspoon ground cinnamon

A pinch of salt

115g sultanas

350g currants

75g mixed peel

50g glacé cherries (chopped)

1–2 tablespoons milk, to mix

225g natural marzipan or almond paste
(see below)

Approximately 4 tablespoons apricot
jam

1 egg yolk, beaten

FOR THE ALMOND PASTE

75g caster sugar

75g icing sugar, plus extra for dusting

350g ground almonds

1 egg, beaten

Juice of ½ lemon

3 drops of almond extract

FOR THE YELLOW ICING

85g icing sugar

1 tablespoon water

2–3 drops of yellow food colouring

Easter wasn't Easter without simnel cake. I once asked Dad why there were eleven marzipan balls and he explained they represented Jesus's apostles, minus Judas. Dad traditionally closed the shop every Good Friday to go to church and we always went for a family walk along the Wey Navigation Canal collecting pussy willow for Mum. Easter Saturday was one of the busiest days as customers bought simnel cakes, hot cross buns, chocolate Easter eggs and figurines.

Preheat the oven to 160ºC/gas mark 3. Grease an 18cm round cake tin that is at least 7cm deep and line it with baking parchment.

If you are using almond paste, prepare this first. Mix the sugar and almonds together with beaten egg, lemon juice and almond extract. Knead the mixture on a board dusted with icing sugar until the ingredients are well blended. Divide the mixture into 3 equal portions. Roll out 2 of these into 18cm circles to fit the cake tin. Divide the remaining amount into 11 equal portions and roll these between your hands into 11 balls, cover them with cling film and set aside.

To make the cake, cream the sugar and butter together thoroughly. Add the eggs gradually, plus 1–2 tablespoons flour if the mixture shows signs of curdling.

Sift the flour, spices and salt into a large bowl. Add the sultanas, currants, peel and cherries. Softly mix the flour and fruit mixture into the creamed mixture, adding a little milk, if required. Aim for a soft consistency.

Place half of the mixture in the tin and flatten out the top. Place 1 circle of marzipan or almond paste on top. Put the remaining cake mixture on top of the marzipan or almond paste and smooth out the top. Place the tin on a baking sheet and bake for 1 hour, then reduce the temperature to 150ºC/gas mark 2 and bake for 2–2½ hours or until a skewer inserted into the centre of the cake comes out clean. When the cake is baked, allow it to cool completely.

Preheat the grill to a medium setting. Gently heat the apricot jam in a pan until it is warm, or in a microwave for 1 minute until it is soft. Brush the top of the cake with the warm apricot jam. Place the second circle of marzipan or almond paste on top. Decorate around the top of the cake with the 11 marzipan balls. Brush the marzipan on the top of the cake with egg yolk, then place it under the grill until the marzipan colours a little. Keep an eye on the cake while it is under the grill so it doesn't burn.

To make the yellow icing, mix the icing sugar, water and yellow food colouring. Decorate the centre of the top of the cake with a little yellow icing. Tie a yellow ribbon around the cake to finish.

sweet delights

chapter five

Smashing the Oven
Sweet Satisfying Rewards

A woman in her late forties with hefty hips peered at the tray of custard tarts behind the counter.

"Can I help you?" Frankie asked.

"I'd like to speak to the manager," the lady said in a broad Scottish accent.

"I'm the co-owner, along with Peter." Frankie shifted on her feet. She was always on guard when anyone asked this question.

"Let me introduce myself. My name is Agnes Robertson and I'm the new EHO for this area. You can call me Ms Robertson."

EHO – the three letters guaranteed to make Mum's stomach flip over; they stood for Environmental Health Officer (or Evil Horrid Officer, as some preferred). Frankie's heart sank. A visit from the EHO meant more work, more stress and the inevitable extra costs for modern equipment required by ever changing European legislation.

The EHO's eyes darted around the shop. One minute she stared at the wholemeal bread as if she was a Michelin Guide inspector, then she examined the homemade chocolates as if they were poison. It didn't matter how appetizing the chocolates and cakes appeared, the expression on the EHO's face was always one of utter disdain. "I'm not going to inspect your premises today but I am here to inform you that I will be revisiting in two weeks for my first inspection."

"Would you like a cup of tea?" Frankie asked.

"No, thank you. However, I must give you the official notice for my visit." She handed a note to Frankie, eyes fixed on a glass tray filled with fruit and wholemeal scones. "I have very high expectations and very high standards. In fact, I have higher standards than the average EHO, but I'm also very fair."

Mum nodded. Here we go again, she thought. Last time, the EHO demanded new fridges and flooring. What would it be this time? And where on earth would the extra money come from? Dad worked as hard as he could, but there was only so much money to be made from cakes, bread and chocolates. In the seventies, inspectors had time for tea and conversation but, during the eighties, the EHO visits caused increasing pressure and strain, which mounted in the following decade with the introduction of tougher legislation for family-run businesses. Suddenly, inspectors changed into space age suits and came armed with clipboards, cameras and thermometers, plus a long list of legal requirements.

However much time we all spent cleaning the shop, it could never be clean enough for an inspection. I remember the atmosphere in the bakehouse changed from being one of calm to being highly stressed prior to an inspection. Mum used cotton buds and good old-fashioned Milton sterilizing liquid to get into tricky places in fridges. Johnny booked time off work to help by scrubbing floors and doing a clean sweep of the problem areas such as the store room. After leaving school, Johnny had worked in the shop for several years before joining the police and living nearby. Johnny's skills as a senior police officer meant he had a great eye for detail. The store room, at the back of the bakehouse, was packed with ingredients and blackened cake tins that resembled baking utensils from the Middle Ages. Johnny wanted all the ancient equipment removed but Dad wanted to keep all his 'little treasures', right down to the mustard spoons from his parents' tea shop. The matter remained undecided while we busied ourselves with the rest of the cleaning.

Fuby, who works in education, and I helped to clean the cake cabinets and shelves while Gordon, the MD of a drinks company, mucked in; together, all of the family spent hours preparing for the day of reckoning, when Dad's traditional skills and work practices would be put under the microscope by the EHO once more. Over the years, different regulations were introduced, covering everything from small equipment such as piping bags and knives, to marble slabs, fridges and flooring. Even Dad's faithful radio, which kept him company in the early mornings, was targeted for being a dust collector. Despite all the grief, the inspectors were always satisfied.

In the end, it wasn't the fridges or the flooring that caused the major problem. By the nineties, Mum and Dad, like many small-business owners, struggled to make a profit as business rates soared and supermarkets arrived on the high street. International coffee chains transformed Weybridge High Street.

Peter's health took a turn for the worse in the nineties when he collapsed in the bakehouse, suffering from a heart attack. Dad's health problems and the mounting legislation meant Mum and Dad were under increasing pressure at a time in their lives when they should have been taking it easy. Yet the majority of our customers did not detect any issues. The traditional tea shop service continued, Dad rose early every day to bake bread and cakes as

he had always done… until January 2000, when finally, it became time to shut up shop.

By then, I was working for *The Sunday Times* as Assistant Editor of *Style* magazine. I had the most delightful two-year-old, Lara, with striking strawberry blonde hair. The competitive newspaper office couldn't have been more different from the cosy family bakery in Weybridge where Mum and Dad were shutting up shop after forty two years in business. The final day is etched in my memory. When I arrived at *Peter's* for the last time, there was a sign on the door announcing the closure, thanking people for their custom. It was horrible to read. It was a Saturday afternoon and, typical of Dad, it had been a normal trading day. The pressure was on because the shop had to be cleared out by Monday. There were no cake displays left in the windows, the glass counters lay bare, the fridges were switched off and empty, the dark chocolates gone from the cabinet. There was no gentle hum of conversation from the café, no clattering of cutlery, no scent of baking, only the lingering sterile scent of cleaning liquids. This wasn't how it was meant to be, yet I knew it was time for Mum and Dad to retire. Dad was seventy and had increasing health problems. When the lease came up, none of my siblings nor I wanted to take over the family shop. We all had our careers and saw no future in cakes.

The new café owner asked Dad to take out the oven. It took a lot longer to destroy than anyone expected. Dad needed Johnny and several burly men to help over two to three days. Dad wasn't surprised at how hard a job it had been. The oven had been a 'solid friend' he said. My lasting image is of the three men smashing it with hammers and chisels.

At the end, all that remained was a dirty, empty space. Dad got down on his knees and scrubbed the greasy floor. Usually, his apron was dotted with ingredients, but on this last day he was covered in dust. Our family had been pastry chefs for over one hundred years but the line now appeared to have finished. The oven was gone, the last of the family tea shops had closed.

When the job was done, the men washed their hands and Mum brought out some tea, flapjacks and slabs of farmhouse fruitcake. "This was the last batch of cakes from that oven," Peter said. No-one uttered a word. We sat there and gorged ourselves until they were all gone. I remember wanting to savour the taste of the last flapjack forever: the sweet oats that always made me feel at home, the farmhouse cake stuffed full of fruit. The men finished off the cakes and drank tea from big mugs reserved for tradesmen. The china had been packed away, the oven gone, the cakes all eaten.

Farmhouse cake and flapjacks are the perfect fuel to repay hard work and give an energy boost. All the following recipes are for cakes that make satisfying rewards after strenuous jobs. A rock cake or slice of treacle tart are ideal treats while at work or simply when you feel you deserve it.

RUM TRUFFLES

MAKES 12-15

175g cake crumbs

1 tablespoon cocoa, sifted

25g caster sugar

2 tablespoons apricot or raspberry jam

1–1½ tablespoons rum

2 tablespoons chocolate vermicelli

Cake crumbs and rum are the essential ingredients in rum truffles. Dad kept all the cake trimmings, which he used in the truffles along with a few other cakes requiring crumbs. As a child I loved rolling the truffles in the chocolate vermicelli. Gordon likes these because of the combination of chocolate and alcohol.

Mix the cake crumbs, cocoa and sugar together. Beat the jam and rum until the mixture is smooth, then mix it into the crumb mixture to form a soft paste.

Divide the mixture into 12–15 equal portions and form each one of these into a ball the size of a medium cherry tomato. Roll each ball in the chocolate vermicelli and place it in a paper case.

baker's tip

Replace the rum with 2 tablespoons jam to make 'jam truffles' that are great for children's parties. If you don't have spare cake crumbs, use shop-bought Madeira or plain sponge to make some.

FRANKIE'S FLAPJACKS

MAKES APPROXIMATELY 32

320g butter

330g caster sugar

4 tablespoons golden syrup

200g condensed milk

500g porridge oats

Flapjacks are one of my favourites. When friends came to tea in *Peter*'s I often chose a flapjack while they picked a tray of cream cakes. Mum adapted Dad's crispier recipe using condensed milk, making the flapjack stickier. She still makes regular batches which friends describe as 'The best flapjack ever'. These are perfect when you want a sweet lift.

Preheat the oven to 150ºC/gas mark 2. Line a 20 x 25cm tin with silicone.

Melt the butter, sugar and syrup in a large saucepan. When the sugar is dissolved, take the pan off the heat and add the condensed milk. Mix in the oats until they are well covered.

Put the mixture in the prepared tin and level off the surface. Bake for 10–15 minutes until the top is lightly browned. Remove the flapjack from the tin, still on the silicone and, while warm, cut the flapjack into 16, then cut each piece in half to make 32 pieces.

baker's tip

You can add 50g sultanas, cranberries or chopped nuts to the mixture with the oats, if desired.

smashing the oven

ROCK CAKES

MAKES 10-12

225g plain flour

A pinch of salt

1 teaspoon baking powder

½ teaspoon mixed spice

½ teaspoon grated nutmeg

110g butter, plus extra for greasing

25g mixed peel

50g currants (or use raisins and/or sultanas)

110g caster sugar, plus extra for sprinkling

1 egg, beaten

1 tablespoon milk, to mix

Rock cakes were popular with builders and tradesmen who wanted a filling snack. Being a cross between a sponge and a scone, a rock cake made by Dad was never rock hard. They are easy to make. Mum adds extra spices to hers to give them an added kick, as you can to suit your taste.

Preheat the oven to 180°C/gas mark 4. Grease a baking sheet and line it with baking parchment.

Sift the flour, salt, baking powder and mixed spices in a bowl. Rub in the butter until the mixture resembles fine breadcrumbs.

Stir in the peel, currants and sugar. Make a well in the centre, put the beaten egg and milk into this well and stir, then gradually incorporate the dry ingredients from around the edges of the well until everything is mixed. Add more milk if the mix is too dry to form a dough.

Use 2 forks to place the mix on the parchment. Bake for 15–20 minutes or until light golden. Sprinkle over the sugar when baked.

baker's tip

Bake these cakes lightly – for a short amount of time – or you may get real rock cakes.

smashing the oven

FARMHOUSE FRUITCAKE

SERVES 8–10

50g raisins

50g currants

50g sultanas

50g mixed peel

3 tablespoons Calvados (or a brandy alternative)

175g butter, plus extra for greasing

175g demerara sugar

450g plain flour

1 teaspoon bicarbonate of soda

2 eggs

275ml milk

Granulated sugar, to sprinkle

Farmhouse fruitcake was a regular batch cake, one of the tea shop originals, sold as a whole cake rather than in slices. It is moist and not as heavy as a rich fruitcake. It was popular with Weybridge ladies who knew it not only lasted for over a week but it improved with age.

The night before you make the cake, put the dried fruit into a bowl and add 2 tablespoons of the Calvados. Cover the bowl and leave the fruit to soak overnight so that the flavour of the brandy infuses the dried fruit.

When you're ready to prepare the cake, preheat the oven to 160°C/ gas mark 3. Grease the base and sides of a 20cm round cake tin that is 8cm deep.

Cream the butter and sugar together (bear in mind that the creamed mixture won't be as light and fluffy as it would be if using caster sugar). Mix in a third of the flour with the bicarbonate of soda, followed by an egg and then another third of the flour, then the final egg followed by the remaining flour. At this stage, the cake batter will be quite dry. Blend the milk and remaining Calvados into the mixture until you have a smooth batter, then fold in the dried fruit carefully.

Ease the mixture into your prepared cake tin. Bake for 1 hour, then cover the tin with baking parchment or kitchen foil and bake for a further 25–30 minutes or until a skewer inserted into the centre of the cake comes out clean. Sprinkle some granulated sugar on top to decorate while the cake is still hot from the oven.

TREACLE TART

SERVES 8

1 quantity of sweet shortcrust pastry
(see page 133)

560ml golden syrup

175g sliced white bread or dry (1-day-
old) scones, grated (you'll have
approximately 90g breadcrumbs)

2 teaspoons freshly squeezed lemon
juice

Treacle tart with cream was part of my childhood, like a loyal friend.
One customer, a doctor, occasionally bought four treacle tarts to share
with staff at the local hospital, St Peter's, in Chertsey. When Dad had
to go to the hospital, the same doctor greeted him and looked after him.
Mum often gave cakes and flapjacks to the doctors and nurses while
Dad was admitted.

Preheat the oven to 180°C/gas mark 4.

Line a 20cm tart tin with the sweet shortcrust pastry. Place the tin in the
refrigerator to allow the pastry to rest for 30 minutes.

Warm the golden syrup in a bowl set over a pan of simmering water in
order to make it thin enough to pour freely. Gradually stir the syrup into
the breadcrumbs to make a thick and consistent mixture. Blend the lemon
juice into the filling.

Spoon the filling into the pastry case to a depth of 1cm. Bake for
approximately half an hour.

baker's tip

Prepare the mixture for the filling the night before you
intend to bake the tart, to allow the breadcrumbs to
absorb the syrup and lemon juice. Occasionally, Peter
added 50g crushed almonds and sultanas to the mixture.

smashing the oven

chapter six

Little Pieces of Heaven
Edible Gifts

Dad told me he got his first real taste for homemade chocolates in December 1944 at the age of thirteen, when his Uncle Charlie showed him a box of chocolates he'd made as a Christmas present. It was wartime and there was rationing but, even so, Uncle Charlie tempted him with the most exquisite collection of handmade chocolates Dad had ever seen. The white box had the name of the family tea shop, *Beti's*, inscribed in gold lettering. Inside, plain dark chocolates were arranged in neat rows in individual brown ruffled cases, just as I remember them in *Peter's* gold boxes. Dad eyed up the different shapes and assortment of decorations: coconut, pistachio, almond, rose petal, violet, ginger. He inhaled the heady combination of sweet scents – rose combined with coconut, almond and ginger, all mixed up. He couldn't decide which chocolate to pick. Dad wondered where Uncle Charlie had got the chocolate and dainty decorations from during the war. When he plucked up the courage to ask, Uncle Charlie whispered, "We have ways and means, son. When you've been in the cake and chocolate business as long as I have no-one can stop me from doing what I do best!" Dad told me Charlie was a handsome man, olive-skinned with sparkling blue eyes. He wore a smart camel overcoat and smelled of cigar smoke. "Go on then lad, help yourself!" Uncle Charlie took a puff from his cigar.

Peter picked a peppermint cream – a round, dark chocolate decorated with three dark lines on top – and let it melt in his mouth. He savoured the sharp sweetness of the peppermint and the bitterness of the dark chocolate. He had not tasted anything like it before. The chocolate, with its high cocoa content, was rather rich for a boy's taste buds, but the peppermint fondant was soft and smooth on his tongue. "Fancy another one? Go on," Uncle Charlie encouraged. Peter chose the Brazil nut, bit into the chocolate and crunched. "What do you think? Fancy learning how to make them? You'd be popular at school!"

Dad asked, "Are they hard to make?"

"There's a real art to it," said Uncle Charlie. "You need a delicate touch and a lot of patience. But you have chocolate flowing through your veins, lad. And bread. And cakes. Our family have been making chocolates and cakes since, well, forever."

Dad, like his forebears, learned how to make chocolates by watching and practising. There were no ancient hand-bound recipe books full of cryptic squiggles. Dad simply learned how to be a chocolatier in his grandmother's tea shop, *Beti's*, by standing next to Uncle Charlie and watching him for hours at a time. He was never bored as Uncle Charlie showed him how to turn the brick-sized slabs of dark chocolate into 'little pieces of heaven' as Charlie called them.

Dad told me he loved to watch how the huge chunks of chocolate melted into a pool of velvet liquid. He inhaled the rich scent as Uncle Charlie stirred and tasted until the right amount of chocolate had been applied. There were always rewards. Uncle Charlie allowed him to lick any bowls or spoons and, if he was very lucky, he was given a chocolate or two. I've often thought Dad's destiny was predetermined. When he started working in his parents' tea shop, he made chocolates as if it was expected of him. When he opened *Peter's* he made precisely the same-flavoured chocolates as Uncle Charlie. Peter always saw himself as a baker *and* confectioner.

OVER THE YEARS, Peter progressed from making delicate handmade chocolates to creating Easter eggs and magnificent moulded chocolates in different shapes and sizes. Word spread around that if you wanted homemade chocolates or chocolate animal figurines you travelled to *Peter's*.

During the forty two years Peter ran the tea shop he received some strange requests. One of the most challenging was the order made by a Weybridge businesswoman in the eighties. "I'd like three hundred chocolate fish," she said. Frankie looked up from a gold box that she'd been filling with homemade chocolates. Half were peppermint creams, half were pistachios. This was a special order for 'my little spinsters' as Mum described two of the Weybridge regulars who wore hats and gloves in summer and winter. "Is that possible?" The businesswoman peered at a chocolate fish in the cabinet. "I love the fact that you can see the tiny scales." She took a step closer to the cabinet and squinted at the six-inch fish.

Mum's first thought was to consider whether or not Dad had the time and energy to make three hundred chocolate fish when she knew for a fact he only had one mould and a mountain of Easter egg orders. Her voice faltered. "Three hundred is rather a lot of fish. Have you got a special event coming up?"

"A press launch, but I'm afraid it's all a bit hush-hush. In fact, you mustn't mention it to a soul." Frankie frowned.

An order for three hundred chocolate fish would be good for business, but Peter had enough orders in the book to keep him working flat out until Good Friday. She walked into the bakehouse where Dad was in the throes of decorating a row of Easter eggs with iced flowers. His white coat was splattered in dark chocolate and there was chocolate on his chin and all over his fingers. He performed the delicate task of making and decorating Easter eggs and figurines with the honed skills of a master chocolatier. At Easter, he smelt of chocolate and hot cross buns. When Dad heard the request he gave a big sigh. "My problem is I've only got one fish mould and one pair of hands."

"I can try to find another one," Frankie said.

Peter sighed again. "We won't find an identical one! My grandparents used it in their tea shop. It's a museum piece. Just tell her I'll do it, we need the business."

Mum tried to source an identical mould without any luck, so Dad made the three hundred fish, one by one, which took over a fortnight. As the days passed I recall the chocolate cabinet slowly filling up with fish. Mum tied a red ribbon around the neck of each one and packed the chocolate moulds into individual gold boxes.

When Mum and Dad retold this story to me after the tea shop had closed I asked if they still had the fish mould. Dad went up to the loft and returned with it clasped in his hands. "Shall we make one?" he said. During all the years I'd watched Dad make chocolate Easter eggs and animal figurines, I'd never made a single one. My time had finally come.

IN THIS CHAPTER I explain how Peter made the chocolate fish. In these days of internet shopping, it is a lot easier to source all sorts of chocolate moulds than it was when Frankie was looking. This chapter also includes other homemade edible gifts. The selection is inspired by some of the most popular products in *Peter's*.

edible gifts

FRANKIE'S FUDGE

MAKES 30 PIECES

900g granulated sugar
285ml water
50g butter, plus extra for greasing
397g can condensed milk
1 teaspoon vanilla extract

Dad occasionally made fudge in the bakehouse, but this became Mum's domain when she retired. Friends and family would constantly ask for her fudge, and she satisfied their cravings by making batches and filling little bags to give away as presents – especially at Christmas.

Grease a 20 x 20cm square cake tin.

Place the sugar and water in a large saucepan. Add the butter and condensed milk. Simmer, stirring occasionally, for about 45 minutes until the mixture thickens. To test if it has cooked enough, drop a small amount of the mixture into a glass of cold water. If a ball forms, it is ready.

Take the pan off the heat and add the vanilla extract. Beat with a wooden spoon until the mixture thickens to a thick pouring consistency. Pour the mixture into the prepared cake tin and leave it for roughly 1 hour to set. Once it has set, cut it into 30 pieces.

baker's tip

If you prefer a creamier fudge, halve the amount of sugar to 450g. You can adapt this vanilla fudge with 25g chopped walnuts or sultanas or 1 teaspoon coffee essence.

little pieces of heaven

CHOCOLATE FISH

MAKES 1

Dark chocolate (the amount you need will depend on the size of your mould), broken into pieces

Dad made a variety of chocolate figurines and Easter eggs. I liked the chocolate chicks and the large chocolate rabbit. The chocolate fish was distinctive because of the tiny scales and it is particularly special to me because Dad showed me how to make it.

For this recipe (and for any moulded chocolates) it is best to use proper cocoa-rich confectionery chocolate. Peter always used Belgian chocolate. Regarding moulds, my advice is to choose one made up of two plastic halves that form a single unit once joined with clips. There will be an obvious opening in which to pour chocolate.

Gently melt enough chocolate to fill your mould in a bowl set over a pan of simmering water. You need to prevent water vapour (steam) from coming into contact with the chocolate, which would affect the texture and appearance of the chocolate once it has dried. A bowl that fits snugly over the pan will help to keep the steam away from the chocolate as it melts. Peter used a purpose-built hot-air bain marie, which has been in the family for decades.

Once molten, the chocolate needs to be tempered, by which process the chocolate is turned continuously to ensure absolute consistency of the distribution of molecules within the chocolate. Pour the chocolate onto a marble or similar work surface and, using two large metal palette knives, fold and turn it over itself repeatedly. As the chocolate cools, it will thicken. When it has the consistency of thick custard, scrape it off the work surface and place it back into the bowl.

Place the bowl back over the pan of simmering water and allow the chocolate to melt again. Repeat the tempering process 2 or 3 times to ensure absolute consistency of texture. The chocolate will be ready to use when it runs freely but slowly from a palette knife.

Slowly pour the chocolate into the mould using a small soup ladle until the mould is half full. Tap the mould on a solid surface a number of times to ensure the chocolate has reached every crevice within. Swirl the chocolate around the mould, then pour in more melted chocolate until the mould is almost full, all the while tapping the mould on a solid surface – you should see air bubbles slowly being released. Once no more bubbles are apparent, upturn the mould, gently tapping the side with a palette knife to release any excess chocolate. When the chocolate runs as a drip it is a sign that the chocolate has coated the mould and will set. Place the mould aside in a cool place with the aperture uppermost (to prevent the setting chocolate from blocking the filling hole) for at least a

baker's tip

A mould must be spotless before you pour in chocolate. Peter sterilized moulds in boiling water, let them dry naturally, then polished the insides with cotton wool. The more you polish, the better the shine on the chocolate. Mum handled the figurines in fine silk gloves.

little pieces of heaven

couple of hours, ideally overnight, to allow the chocolate to set. Do not refrigerate the chocolate.

Reheat the chocolate and repeat the tempering-and-pouring process in order to provide a second layer of chocolate within the first. This second coating should be slightly cooler than the first in order not to melt the first layer. There is no need to be as repetitive with the tapping as before because the release of air bubbles creates an attractive, smooth surface, which is only important on the outer layer. While it is essential for the first coating to cool with the opening uppermost, the second coating should be left to cool with the mould standing the right way up (on parchment paper). In this way some of the cooling chocolate will collect at the base to provide stability for the finished figure.

Once the chocolate has set, carefully undo the clips. The chocolate should have constricted slightly and, when it is absolutely dry, you can almost hear the 2 halves of the mould snap apart. This will free 1 half of the mould, leaving the chocolate fish in the opposite half. Gently hold the mould by the edges and slowly twist it, allowing the plastic to flex, which should release the chocolate figurine. Carefully remove the chocolate figure, touching the outer layer as little as possible as any fingerprints will remain obvious.

CHOCOLATE PEPPERMINT CREAMS

MAKES ABOUT 40 *

400g baker's fondant or soft fondant icing

½–1 teaspoon peppermint extract (depending on how strong you like your peppermint)

Icing sugar, for sprinkling

200g dark chocolate

*depending on the size and depth of the mould

These were my favourite chocolates, and the first thing Dad made in the shop when he opened it in 1958. He continued to make them into his retirement, right up until his illness, and give them as presents in small gold boxes wrapped with red ribbon. Dad was happiest when making chocolates.

Use a silicone mould for making your peppermint creams. Although the traditional shape is round, feel free to make them in whatever shape mould you have. Silicone moulds can be found online or in good kitchen shops.

If moulds are difficult to find then there are alternative methods. You can roll the fondant into small teaspoon-sized balls and flatten with the back of a fork. Or you can pipe the fondant into teaspoon-sized discs on silicone paper. I find silicone moulds the easiest to use.

If using baker's fondant, place the fondant in a saucepan set over a low heat and stir the fondant until it has melted and resembles a thick custard. Splash in the peppermint extract and stir it in well. Turn off the heat.

If using soft, ready-to-roll fondant icing, put the fondant in a microwave-safe bowl and add 2 tablespoons water. Heat the fondant in the microwave in increments of 15 seconds, each time removing the bowl and stirring the fondant. Continue slowly heating the fondant until you have a liquid consistency. Once the fondant is pourable, add the peppermint extract. Place the fondant into a jug for easy pouring.

Sprinkle some icing sugar into your moulds to prevent the peppermint mixture from sticking to them. You can pour the ready-to-roll fondant into your moulds.

If using baker's fondant either use a funnel or spoon the peppermint mixture into the moulds. Leave the moulds in a cool corner of your kitchen to allow the mixture to cool down, but there's no need to pop them into the refrigerator. They should set within 15–20 minutes. Remove the peppermint creams from the moulds and place them on a plate.

Melt the chocolate in a bowl set over a pan of simmering water. Once it has melted, remove the bowl from the heat. You can now dip the creams into the chocolate. For my father's traditional recipe, you dip the whole circle into the chocolate. Place each circle of fondant, one by one, on a chocolate-dipping fork, dip it in the melted chocolate, then lift it out and place it on a baking sheet to dry. Gently dab a fork onto the top of the chocolate as it cools. This should create three parallel lines across the top of each chocolate peppermint cream.

little pieces of heaven

HEART-SHAPED BISCUITS

Perfect for Valentine's Day or a romantic teatime treat, these biscuits are made with the same mixture used for the animal biscuits and are coated with a thin layer of red regal icing. Dad made them every Valentine's Day and they sold quickly. Mum created a special window containing heart-shaped cakes, fruit flans and biscuits for the occasion.

200g butter

200g caster sugar

2 eggs (or 1 egg, 1 yolk – you need 75g), beaten

400g plain flour

1 teaspoon baking powder

Large pinch of salt

3 tbsp apricot jam

200g red ready-to-roll icing

200g dark chocolate

depending on the size of your cutter

Preheat the oven to 180°C/gas mark 4. Line a couple of baking sheets with baking parchment.

Cream the butter and sugar together until the mixture is light and fluffy. Add the eggs, then stir in the flour, baking powder and salt. Gently but thoroughly mix to form a dough. Wrap the dough in cling film and chill in the refrigerator for 30 minutes.

Roll out the dough to a thickness of 7mm. Using a heart-shaped cutter, cut out your shapes. Reroll and cut the trimmings. Transfer the shapes onto the prepared baking sheets and bake for 10–12 minutes until light brown. Leave the biscuits to cool on the baking sheet.

Meanwhile, gently heat the apricot jam in a small pan until warm or in a microwave for 1 minute until soft. Once the biscuits are cool, brush the surface of each biscuit with a small amount of warm apricot jam.

Roll out the icing to a thickness of about 2.5mm. Using the same heart-shaped cutter, cut out the same number of icing hearts as you have biscuit hearts and place one onto each biscuit over the warm jam. Set aside on the baking sheet.

Melt the chocolate in a bowl set over a pan of simmering water, then take the bowl off the heat. To dip each biscuit, place it on a fork, place a finger from the other hand on top to steady the biscuit and dip it into the chocolate so that its base and sides are covered. As you lift the biscuit out of the bowl, drag it against the side of the bowl to remove excess chocolate. Place it on a piece of baking parchment, chocolate-side down, to set. When the chocolate has set, the parchment paper will peel off easily, leaving the chocolate behind on the biscuit.

baker's tip

If you want to add a message to a loved one on the biscuit, adapt the size of the cutter to allow space for the lettering you have in mind and pipe the message directly onto the front of the biscuit, or onto the layer of icing, using either 25g white royal icing or melted chocolate.

DAMSON JAM

MAKES 10–12 X 450g JARS

2.7kg damsons
1.5 litres water
2.7kg granulated sugar

Making homemade jam was both a family and tea shop tradition. Dad made strawberry jam for the shop. Mrs Reece, from Artistic Treasures next door, always ordered ten jars because it sold out so quickly. Johnny has a damson tree in his cottage garden, so Mum makes damson jam using the fruit from his tree.

Place the washed fruit in a pan with the water, which should almost cover the fruit. Bring to the boil, then simmer gently for about 30 minutes until the fruit is cooked.

Now add the sugar. Stir it in over a low heat until it is dissolved. Bring the fruit back to the boil and boil briskly until set, removing stones as they rise to the surface with a slotted spoon. To test for a set, take the pan off the heat, spoon a few drops of the jam onto a plate and place it in the refrigerator to cool it quickly. Once it is cold, press it with a little finger. If a wrinkled skin forms on the jam, it is set. If it doesn't wrinkle, return the pan to heat and boil briskly for a few minutes, then test again.

Place the jam in sterilized, warm jars. While it is still hot, cover the surface of the jam in each jar with a circle of wax paper. Immediately seal the jars.

VICTORIA PLUM JAM

MAKES 7 X 450g JARS

1.8kg Victoria plums, halved and stoned
425ml water
1.8kg granulated sugar

This is another lovely homemade jam and it works particularly well in the chocolate cream slices (see page 91).

Place the fruit and water in a pan and simmer for 15–20 minutes until the plums are soft.

Add the sugar and stir until it is dissolved. Then boil the mixture rapidly for 15–20 minutes until the jam is set. (See the recipe above for information on how to test for a set.)

Take the pan off the heat, skim the surface with a skimming ladle and pour the jam into sterilized, warm jars. Cover the surface of the jam in each jar with a circle of wax paper and seal while the jam is hot.

SEVILLE ORANGE MARMALADE

MAKES 8–10 X 450g JARS

1.35kg Seville oranges
Juice of 3 lemons
3.4 litres water
2.7kg granulated sugar

Dad made marmalade in January and February when the Seville oranges were in season. Mr Brockwell, from the local fruit and veg shop, would deliver them. I recall the large metal preserving pan Dad filled with the bubbling orange mixture and hundreds of marmalade jars lining the shelves.

Scrub the fruit well. Cut each orange in half and squeeze out the juice and pips. Cut the orange pieces in half again, peel them and cut out the thicker pith. Chop the peel finely. Place the pips and pith in a muslin square and tie it closed loosely with kitchen string.

Place the orange and lemon juice, chopped peel and water in a preserving pan or large saucepan. Hang the muslin bag from the side of the pan, ensuring it is immersed in water.

Bring the liquid to the boil and simmer for 1½–2 hours until the peel is really tender. Remove the muslin bag and squeeze it out into the water very well, so that the pectin in the fruit is released. Discard the muslin bag and its contents.

Add the sugar to the preserving pan and stir to dissolve it over a low heat. When it is dissolved, boil the mixture rapidly for about 20 minutes until the marmalade is set. (See page 121 for information on how to test for a set.)

Take the pan off the heat, skim the surface with a skimming ladle and leave to cool for about ten minutes. Then pour it into sterilized, warm jars. Cover the surface of the marmalade in each jar with a circle of wax paper and seal while hot.

baker's tip

Seville oranges freeze well. Just wash the whole orange and freeze. So if they are in season but you don't have time to make marmalade, buy them and freeze them for up to about 3 months until you are ready.

little pieces of heaven

TOMATO CHUTNEY

MAKES 6–7 X 225g JARS

3.175kg ripe tomatoes, skinned and
  chopped

225g onions, finely chopped

275ml distilled vinegar

A pinch of mixed spice

1 teaspoon cayenne

1½ teaspoons paprika

1 tablespoon salt

350g granulated sugar

Dad grew his own tomatoes at home, but he didn't generate enough
for chutney. Mum made tomato chutney for the shop and as gifts. She
always sourced tomatoes from local markets and farms – years before
shopping locally became a trendy issue.

Place tomatoes and onions in a large pan and cook gently for about half
an hour until the mixture has reduced by roughly one-third. Add half the
vinegar, the spices and the salt and reduce again by one-third for about
half an hour. Add the sugar to the mixture, stir well and add the remaining
vinegar. Cook gently for a further half an hour to reduce again, until the
mixture has a fairly thick consistency. Place the hot chutney in sterilized
jars. Cover the surface of the chutney in each jar with a circle of wax
paper and seal while the chutney is hot.

FRANKIE'S HOT CHUTNEY

MAKES 10 X 450g JARS

1.1 litres wine vinegar

1.8kg Bramley apples, peeled and
  chopped

450g onions, chopped

50g crushed garlic

100g grated fresh root ginger

225g seedless raisins, chopped

225g mustard seeds, crushed to a
  powder using a mortar and pestle

450g dark brown sugar

550ml water

225g fresh hot red chillies (or 100g
  dried chillies)

100g sea salt

This chutney wasn't sold in the tea shop. This is Mum's hot chutney,
a spicy accompaniment to a curry that she serves with a side dish or
main course.

Put the wine vinegar in a large pan with apples, onions, garlic, ginger,
raisins and powdered mustard seed. Boil for 5 minutes, then reduce the
heat and simmer.

Dissolve the sugar in the water in a separate pan and add the chillies and
salt. Stir this mixture into the fruity and spicy mixture and simmer for an
hour or until it reaches a chutney consistency. Ensure you stir the
chutney well towards the end of cooking to avoid the mixture sticking.

Pour the chutney into sterilized warm jars. Cover the surface of the
chutney with a circle of wax paper and seal while the chutney is hot.

edible gifts

ALMOND PETIT FOURS

MAKES APPROXIMATELY 12

Rice paper

1½ egg whites, plus 1 extra for washing

110g ground almonds

50g caster sugar

½ teaspoon rose water

1 egg, beaten

FOR THE GLAZE

1 tablespoon milk

2 teaspoons caster sugar

TO DECORATE

Angelica, green or red glacé cherries,
walnuts or half almonds

Dad made a variety of petit fours, sold in gold boxes tied with red ribbon. His trademark petit fours were almond fancies decorated with a sliced almond, glacé cherry or angelica, for which I give the recipe here. He also made oval-shaped chocolate Dutch macaroons, chocolate hollandaise and stuffed dates. These were all sold by weight using old-fashioned scales and made ideal gifts.

Preheat the oven to 150°C/gas mark 2. Place a sheet of rice paper on a baking sheet.

Beat the egg whites in a bowl. Add the ground almonds, sugar and rose water. Now add the beaten egg gradually to make a soft paste.

Put the mixture into a piping bag fitted with a 9mm star-shaped nozzle. Pipe stars that are 2.5cm in diameter onto the rice paper on the baking sheet. Decorate the tops of the stars with glacé cherries, almonds, walnuts and/or angelica – or use your preferred decoration. Brush each piece well with egg white. Bake for 10–15 minutes.

Now prepare the glaze. Warm the milk in a saucepan, add the sugar and stir it in until it has dissolved. Brush this on top of each warm petit four to give it a nice glaze. Leave the petit fours to set on a wire rack.

edible gifts

MARZIPAN FRUITS

MAKES ABOUT 30 FRUITS

500g marzipan
Food colouring in orange, yellow,
    green and red

TO DECORATE

Cloves, stalks for the apples,
    pears and bananas
Cloves heads (without seeds) for the
    oranges and lemons
Melted dark chocolate, for the bananas

Dad transformed marzipan into colourful miniature fruits: apples, bananas, pears, oranges and more. My nephew, Nick, loves them. For his tenth birthday Dad made him a special birthday cake decorated with marzipan fruits. I doubt any other child has ever had a cake quite like that!

Divide the marzipan into 5 x 100g pieces.

Oranges Colour a portion of marzipan orange using roughly 2–3 drops of orange food colouring, then divide the coloured marzipan into 6 pieces. Roll each of these into the ball shape of an orange, moulding the shape between the palms of your hands. Gently rub each piece over a grater to give the surface the appearance of orange peel. Press in a clove head.

Bananas Colour a portion of marzipan yellow with 2–3 drops of food colouring, then divide the mixture into 6 equal pieces. Roll each of these lengthwise into a sausage shape, then press in the ends so that they taper. Push the 2 ends in the same direction to give the marzipan the shape of a banana. Using a cocktail stick, decorate with a thin chocolate line on 1 side (the other will be resting on the board or plate). You could add a little colouring on the end and tip, too, if you like. Press in a clove as a stalk.

Apples Colour a portion of marzipan green with 2–3 drops of food colouring, then divide the mixture into 6 equal portions. Shape each of these as an apple by rolling it into a ball and squashing it inwards slightly at the top and bottom. Paint 1 side with neat pale red food colouring to give the appearance of ripeness. Press a clove in as an apple stalk, which will help to create the depression at the top of the apples.

Pears Colour a portion of the marzipan green with 2–3 drops of food colouring, then divide the mixture into six equal portions. Shape each of these as a pear by rolling them into a ball as you did for the apples, then tapering 1 end. Press in a clove as a pear stalk.

Lemons Colour a portion of marzipan yellow with 2–3 drops of food colouring, then divide the mixture into 6 equal portions. Shape each of these as a lemon by rolling it into a ball and gently easing each end out a little. Gently grate the surface of each piece to give it the appearance of lemon peel. Press in a clove head.

baker's tip
If you like making fruits you can progress
to making little animals and figures.

little pieces of heaven

chapter seven

Baking With My Father
Bread, Pastry and Savoury Specials

When I asked Dad if he'd teach me his classic recipes he suggested a loaf of white bread as the first masterclass. One Sunday, I arrived at the family home in Weybridge with Lara and Joe, clutching a bag containing three aprons, a bag of flour, a tub of margarine and some yeast. I wasn't sure whether or not I needed any other ingredients to bake a loaf of white bread but this was a start.

Dad was wearing his bakehouse apron, still splattered with bits of chocolate and cheese. He was sitting on his stool in the homely kitchen with its marble effect surfaces, stainless steel double oven, primrose yellow painted walls and mugs with 'Nan' and 'Grand-dad' scrawled on them. The one big difference in this otherwise ordinary family kitchen was the large number of kitchen utensils, amassed over the family's hundred or so years of tea shop trading.

"Get your apron on, then," Dad said in a tone that meant 'no messing'. I felt like an army cadet on duty. Mum whisked the children out of the kitchen to the living room, sensing that today was an important masterclass for the baker and his daughter. For a baker who had made lots of loaves and cakes every day of his working life, just one white loaf was a small job. For me, making my first loaf of bread was a momentous occasion. I was usually the writer, not the baker. As I dug out my notebook and pen, my mobile went off. Dad sighed and rubbed his forehead. "Are you baking or talking?" I decided to ignore the call and switch off the phone. "Right then, measure the flour and margarine," he ordered.

"How much do I need?"

"Let's have eight ounces of flour, half an ounce of margarine," he said with authority, sticking with the old Imperial measurements.

"How do you know?"

"Trust me," he shook his head. "Now, get your hands in the mixture. Come on, get stuck in, get your hands messy."

For the very first time, I wasn't watching Dad make bread or cakes, I was doing it myself. My hands were covered in dough. "Add some more flour," he said, after putting in a finger. "There, that's the right texture. How does that feel?"

"Doughy," I squished the dough off my fingers. Once the mixing and kneading had been done and we'd let the dough 'rest' for a while, I spooned it into an old greased sandwich bread tin Peter used in the bakehouse. He opened the oven door and shook his head again. "This oven isn't as good as the old one." He slid the tray containing the sandwich tin inside and closed the door.

"Great." I brushed down my apron, feeling pleased with myself. I was high on bread making. "How long will it take to bake?" I asked.

"I'll know when it's ready," he said.

"What do you mean?"

"I'll know when it's baked. Trust me."

I glanced at the kitchen clock, which three years ago stopped at 2.48 p.m. I sighed and thought, 'Mum and Dad are getting on'. I made a note of the time the bread went into the oven. I've since learned that the way Dad baked was through a process of relying on his knowledge and instinct rather than recipes and set timings to guide his cooking. Peter never used a timer in over forty years of baking and he was certainly not going to start now. Thirty minutes or so later, he took the bread out of the oven. He shook the loaf out of the tin and knocked it on the base. It sounded hollow.

"If you hear that sound, you know it is baked. Come on, you try it," he said.

"Oh, lovely." I inhaled the doughy smell. I knocked on the base and felt so happy to have made my very first loaf. It wasn't healthy wholemeal, rye, spelt, gluten free or soda bread sprinkled with sunflower seeds. This was a simple white loaf. It smelt divinely doughy.

Several hours later, back home in my own kitchen, I cut the loaf and touched the soft slice. I tasted it and savoured the moment. It may not have been as perfect as the white bread Dad made in the bakehouse, but I didn't expect, or desire, to turn into a master baker overnight. This was my first baking baby step.

As I enjoyed the bread, I pictured Dad in his prime in the bakehouse: healthy and strong with large muscular forearms, pulling a tray of ten loaves out of the oven, with the tray carefully balanced on his trusty metal paddle. Then, I reflected on our first bread-making lesson when, at the age of seventy seven, stooped and bent over the family oven, he pulled out our loaf.

1 A fun baking class with Dad. **2** Lara with pink cottage cake;
the tradition continues. **3** Joe making carrot cake with Dad.
4 Mum shows off her signature lemon drizzle cake.

Since our bread-making session, I found the old oven paddle in the back of the family garage along with a load of other equipment: huge mixing bowls, dough hooks and the proving machine. I've had the oven paddle refurbished with a new handle. This solid friend is a reassuring presence in my kitchen, a reminder of Dad's traditional bread making over so many years.

After that first bread class I turned up regularly with Lara and Joe, to bake the time-honoured tea shop recipes. After bread, we moved on to sweet and savoury pastry, puff pastry and choux pastry. I mixed ingredients and rolled the pastry with an ancient rolling pin under Dad's guidance. Making my first batch of sweet pastry felt like both a miracle and a baking milestone. This was what Dad had always made, but now I was finally learning. We made the classics – everything from custard tarts to cheese omelettes. Mum confessed she had always left the pastry to Dad so when she made her first batch of pastry and quiche Lorraine there was a family lunch to celebrate. Lara and Joe got their hands messy, too, and learned to bake so much younger than me.

Looking back, that first bread-making class didn't just teach me how to make a loaf, it inspired the family to bake. The baker's grandchildren now bake with the kind of confidence that comes from learning with a pastry chef who lived to bake.

WHAT FOLLOWS is a selection of the classic bread and pastry recipes I recorded with Dad, including the simple white loaf, varieties of pastry and the savoury favourites: quiche and Welsh rarebit.

PUFF PASTRY

MAKES 1kg

240g butter, plus extra for greasing
450g plain flour, plus extra for dusting
A pinch of salt
¼ teaspoon cream of tartar
250–300ml water

Puff pastry was part of Dad's life. He made it virtually every day. He used it for a variety of cakes, such as the chocolate cream slices, the palmiers, cream horns and millefeuille. To me, it is magical that these basic ingredients transform into puff pastry and such lovely cakes.

In a large bowl, rub 60g of the butter into the flour. Sprinkle in the salt and the cream of tartar. Gradually pour in the water until the mixture forms into a dough – note that it will be more like a bread dough than shortcrust pastry dough. Slice the remaining butter into slivers and refrigerate these.

On a floured surface, roll out the pastry into a rectangle that is about 3cm thick. Mentally split the rolled dough into 3 sections: left, centre and right. Evenly spread 30g of the butter slivers onto the centre section of the dough, then fold the left end of the pastry over the top. Evenly spread a further 30g of the slivers of butter on top of this folded dough and fold the right end of dough over the top. You should be left with a rectangle shape made up of 3 layers of dough with the slivers of butter separating each layer. Place this on a plate, cover it with cling film and rest it in the refrigerator for a minimum of 15 minutes.

Remove the dough from the refrigerator and, with the folded edges to your left and right, roll it out to a rectangle that is about 3cm thick lengthwise (away from you). Repeat the folding and buttering process as described above, this time folding in top and bottom sections in turn and, again, separating each layer with 30g butter slivers. Place the dough on a plate, cover it with cling film and refrigerate it once again for 15 minutes. Repeat this step once more using the remaining butter. Refrigerate for at least 30 minutes or until needed (you can keep it in the refrigerator for up to 1 week, or freeze it for up to 3 months).

baker's tip

If you don't want your puff pastry to rise excessively – for example, if you're using it for the base of a millefeuille – you need to perforate it at regular intervals prior to baking in order to allow the air to escape from the pastry. Don't worry if you forget to perforate it because you can use the palm of your hand to press down gently on the cooked pastry.

baking with my father

SWEET SHORTCRUST PASTRY

MAKES ENOUGH TO LINE A 20cm TART TIN

100g plain flour, plus extra for dusting
60g butter
½ egg (you need 20g), beaten
40g caster sugar
Pinch of salt

In the mornings, Dad first made the bread dough, followed by the bun dough and cream cakes. He made batches of sweet pastry every day plus he made plain pastry and puff pastry in the afternoons for subsequent days. Dad's pastry was pretty perfect, but I am biased.

Put the flour and butter in a food processor and mix together until the mixture resembles fine breadcrumbs. If using hands, rub the butter and flour together until you have breadcrumbs.

Add the egg to the caster sugar and salt, then stir with a palette knife – this allows the sugar grains to dissolve into the egg so that the sugar is evenly distributed throughout the pastry. Add the egg and sugar mixture to the flour and mix everything together to form a dough. Shape the dough into a round, wrap it in cling film and place in the refrigerator for 30 minutes.

Take the pastry out of the refrigerator about 10 minutes before you need to use it to allow it to reach room temperature, then roll it out on a floured surface to fit a 20cm greased and lined tin. Alternatively, freeze the pastry for up to 1 month.

baker's tip

Always ensure your butter is chilled and cubed before using. Cold hands and a cold bowl will help to make good pastry. If your dough is sticky, sprinkle with flour.

CUSTARD TARTS

MAKES 21 TARTS COOKED
IN A SHALLOW MUFFIN TIN *

FOR THE SHORTCRUST PASTRY

225g plain flour, plus extra for dusting

110g butter, plus extra for greasing

1 egg, beaten

50g caster sugar

½ teaspoon vanilla extract

FOR THE CUSTARD FILLING

40g caster sugar

4 medium egg yolks

½ teaspoon vanilla extract

300ml warm milk

Approximately ½ teaspoon grated
    nutmeg

*or 10–13 tarts cooked in
    aluminium cases

In the bakehouse Dad had a special bench-mounted tart cutter to cut the pastry for the custard tarts. Making these tarts was a fun childhood game. We would cut the pastry cases, Dad filled the tarts with the warm custard filling, then we'd sprinkle the nutmeg on top. These days, my daughter Lara loves making them.

Preheat the oven to 180ºC/gas mark 4. If using a muffin tin, grease the holes and line them carefully with baking parchment.

First, make the shortcrust pastry using the method described on page 133, but adding the vanilla extract to the sugar with the egg. Refrigerate the pastry for 30 minutes wrapped in cling film while you make the custard mixture.

Mix the caster sugar, egg yolks and vanilla extract, then stir in the warm milk until the sugar is fully dissolved.

Roll out the pastry to a depth of 2mm. Using a pastry cutter or saucer, cut out circles of pastry that are slightly larger than the holes in your muffin tin or your foil cases. You may reroll any trimmings, but try to do this only once as the pastry will get tougher the more you roll it.

Pour the custard mixture into the pastry cases, ensuring you leave a 1mm gap at the top to prevent the mixture spilling over. Sprinkle some nutmeg over the custard mixture.

Bake for 25–30 minutes or until the custard is set. It may wobble a little but you can test it by inserting a knife; the custard shouldn't be watery. Allow the tarts to cool to make them easier to remove from the tins – trust me!

baker's tip

Dad used aluminium foil cases, but they can be hard to find these days so use a shallow muffin tray or loose-based tartlet tins. Ensure you roll the pastry to the right thickness (not too thick) and grease your cases, muffin tin holes or tartlet tins to avoid them sticking. If you have a little custard mixture left over it is tasty warmed up and poured over fresh fruit.

baking with my father

APPLE DUMPLINGS

Butter, for greasing

6 tablespoons raisins

2 tablespoons caster sugar, plus extra
for sprinkling

½ teaspoon cinnamon

600g puff pastry (see page 132)

4 small Bramley apples or dessert
apples (I recommend Jazz apples),
peeled and cored

1 egg, beaten

4 cloves

When we had a surplus of apples from the greengrocer or a family
member or friend, Dad made apple dumplings, both to sell and to serve
in the tea room. These dumplings, encased in puff pastry, are stuffed
with a mix of fruits and cinnamon.

Grease a baking sheet.

In a bowl, mix together the raisins, caster sugar and cinnamon.

Roll out the pastry and cut 4 x 20cm circles, each of which should be large
enough to encase each apple. Don't discard the remaining pastry as you
will need this later on.

Place the 4 pastry circles on the prepared baking sheet and stand an apple
in the centre of each pastry circle. Using a teaspoon, place a quarter of the
raisin mixture down the centre of each apple. If the raisins don't reach the
top, add a few more. Bring 4 opposing edges of the pastry to the middle of
the top of the apple to encase the stuffed fruit. With your thumb, push
down the pastry onto the centre.

Using the leftover pastry, cut 4 x 2cm circles, brush 1 side of each of these
with a little beaten egg, then apply 1 of these, egg wash side down, on the
top of each apple and stick it down. This circle covers the gathered pastry
at the top of each dumpling, creating a neat finish. Brush the apples with
egg wash. Sprinkle with some sugar. Place the baking sheet in the
refrigerator and chill the dumplings for 20 minutes.

Preheat the oven to 190ºC/gas mark 5.

Using the point of a sharp knife, twist a little hole into the top of the
pastry on each apple, which will allow the steam to escape during
cooking. Pop a clove into each hole, ensuring that it is not too tight a fit.
Bake for 40–45 minutes or until the pastry is golden brown. If the pastry
begins to look too dark during cooking, loosely cover the apples with
some kitchen foil, removing it a little while before the end of the cooking
to ensure the pastry is crisp.

baker's tip

After the dumplings have been chilled in the refrigerator, leave
them to stand for half an hour at room temperature before baking
otherwise the pastry shrinks. Dessert apples will hold their shape
better than cooking apples and will retain some bite after cooking.

baking with my father

TRADITIONAL APPLE PIE

SERVES 8-10

750g Bramley apples, peeled, cored and sliced

2 tablespoons water

50g caster sugar

8 cloves

1 tablespoon milk, for glazing

Caster sugar, for sprinkling

FOR THE PASTRY

A double quantity of sweet shortcrust pastry (see page 133)

A slice of homemade hot apple pie with cream is like a cuddle. The lunches in *Peter's* may have been described as 'light', but the apple pie with cloves was homely and hearty. When Dad showed me how to make this apple pie I was surprised at how easy it was. Apple pie is often served with custard, but Dad only ever served it with whipped cream or ice cream.

Preheat the oven to 200°C/gas mark 6.

Roll out just over half of the pastry on a lightly floured surface. Use it to line a 20cm pie dish.

Stew the apple slices in the water over a low heat for 5–10 minutes until they soften slightly, stirring occasionally. Place half the stewed apple slices in the pastry-lined dish, then mix in the sugar and cloves. Pile the remaining stewed apple on top.

Roll out the remaining pastry into a circle that is slightly larger than the top of the dish.

Cover the stewed apple with the pastry, trim off any excess pastry and seal the edges. Crimp the pastry around the edges. Prick 2 holes in the top of the pastry, then brush the top with milk.

Bake for 20 minutes, then reduce the temperature to 180°C/gas mark 4 and bake for 20 minutes more or until the pastry turns golden brown. Sprinkle with caster sugar as soon as the pie comes out of the oven. Serve hot or cold (we served it hot in the shop) with fresh whipped cream. In the summer, apple pie is best served cold.

baker's tip

You can add 50g raisins to the apples or swap apples, weight for weight, for other fruit. In *Peter's* we also served apricot or cherry pie.

CHOUX BUNS

MAKES 40

125ml water
50g butter, plus extra for greasing
75g strong plain flour, sifted
2–3 eggs (you need 100g), beaten

FOR THE FILLING AND TOPPING

100g dark chocolate, broken into pieces
300ml whipping cream
1 teaspoon caster sugar (optional)

Dad made choux pastry every day for cream chocolate éclairs. He also made choux pastry for choux buns, chocolate profiteroles and gâteau St Honoré. Once made, he kept the buns in a sealed tin for a few days. My daughter, Lara, loves making choux buns.

It is incredibly important that you measure the ingredients precisely for this recipe. Preheat the oven to 200ºC/gas mark 6. Grease a couple of large baking sheets.

Put the water and butter into a saucepan and bring to the boil, then remove the pan from the heat and add the sifted flour immediately. Beat in the flour until the mixture comes away from the sides of the saucepan. Allow the mixture to cool slightly for a couple of minutes, then gradually beat in the egg until the mixture is smooth and glossy – you may not need to add all of the egg. Stop when the mixture is smooth and glossy but still able to hold a shape.

Put a heaped teaspoonful of the mixture for each bun onto the prepared baking sheet, spacing them 2–3cm apart. Bake for 25 minutes or until the buns take on a nice golden colour. For crispier buns, increase the oven temperature to 220ºC/gas mark 7 halfway through the cooking time. Cool on a wire rack. Pierce each one to allow steam to escape.

Prepare the topping. Melt the chocolate in a bowl set over a pan of simmering water. Once the chocolate has melted, take the bowl off the pan and dip the tops of the buns into the chocolate. Turn them the right way up and place them on a wire rack and allow the chocolate to set.

Now prepare the filling. Whip the cream until it is thick, adding the caster sugar while whipping, if desired, to make the cream a little sweeter.

Cut the chocolated buns in half horizontally and fill them with the fresh cream. Sandwich the two halves of each bun together once it is filled.

baker's tip

If you place a small bowl of boiling water in the oven while you are baking the choux buns or éclairs the steam will give the buns better volume.

baking with my father

CHOCOLATE ÉCLAIRS

MAKES 16–20

125ml water
50g butter
75g strong plain flour, sifted
2–3 eggs (you need 100g), beaten

FOR THE FILLING AND TOPPING

300ml whipping cream
1 teaspoon caster sugar (optional)
150g dark chocolate, broken into pieces

Chocolate éclairs remind me of a rotund priest who had a penchant for these choux buns. When he came into the shop and Mum offered him something to eat he'd say, "I'd like an éclair, my dear!" The phrase stuck in my head, along with the sight of the priest in his cassock enjoying this indulgent treat.

To make chocolate éclairs follow the method instructions for choux buns, opposite, then put the choux paste into a piping bag fitted with a 1cm wide round nozzle. Pipe 10cm lengths onto a baking sheet lined with baking parchment, allowing room to expand. Bake for 20–25 minutes or until the éclairs take on a nice golden colour. Cool on a wire rack. Cut slits in the sides of the éclairs to allow steam to escape.

To make the filling, whip the cream with the caster sugar (if you prefer) until the cream holds its shape. Spoon into a piping bag with a 1cm plain nozzle and carefully fill the éclairs.

Prepare the topping. Melt the chocolate in a bowl set over a pan of simmering water. Once the chocolate has melted, take the bowl off the heat. Dip the top of each éclair into the chocolate, then place it on a wire rack. Leave in a cool place until the chocolate is set. Éclairs are best served soon after making.

baker's tip

Substitute coffee icing for the chocolate topping. Melt 200g white fondant icing with 1 tablespoon Camp Coffee Essence or instant coffee. Dip the buns in the icing. Or make icing sugar topping. Mix 100g icing sugar with 1 tablespoon water and apply with a palette knife.

WHITE SQUARE SANDWICH LOAF

**MAKES 2 X 450g LOAF,
OR 1 X 900g LOAF**

500g super strong premium white flour,
plus extra for dusting

2 teaspoons sugar (optional)

1¼ teaspoons salt

25g margarine, plus extra for greasing

1½ teaspoons fast action dried yeast

300ml warm water

*Dad made loaves of various sizes to sell over the counter. He toasted
the bread for Welsh rarebit and buck rarebit. He also made wholemeal
loaves, white and brown rolls, rye bread, bridge rolls, baps, French
sticks, brioche and croissants.*

*During the bread strikes in the seventies people queued around
the corner for bread, and strangers sneaked around the back of the
bakehouse begging for a loaf. Never was a baker so popular.*

Lightly grease your loaf tin (or a baking sheet).

In a large bowl, mix together the flour, sugar (if using) and salt. Rub in the
margarine and stir in the yeast. Stir in the warm water and mix into a soft
dough by hand. Knead the dough for 5 minutes in a freestanding food
mixer fitted with a dough hook, or turn it out onto a floured surface and
knead well by hand for about 10 minutes. To best achieve this, flatten the
dough with your knuckles and pull both edges apart before folding them
inwards on top of themselves so you have 3 layers of dough. Tightly roll
the dough forwards on top of itself in order to form a giant swiss roll
shape. Keep kneading in this way for 5–10 minutes.

When your dough feels smooth, place it into a lightly oiled bowl. Cover it
with a clean, damp tea towel and leave in a warm place to prove or until it
has almost doubled in size. Peter had a proving cabinet in which to leave
the dough to rise – an airing cupboard has proved fine for me. Be mindful
that the proving stage can take up to 1 hour so don't be in a rush.
Alternatively, leave the dough to rise in a warm corner of the kitchen, but
this will take longer.

Tip your dough onto the floured surface. Divide the dough in half if you
are making 2 small loaves. Shape the dough into a ball, folding the dough
inwards repeatedly until the air is knocked out.

Form the dough into an oblong, flatten out the dough and fold the sides
into the middle. Ensure the join runs along the base and the top is
smooth. Place the dough in the prepared tin or on a baking sheet. Leave
the dough to prove for about 1 hour or until the dough has almost
doubled in size. In the meantime, preheat the oven to 220°C/gas mark 7.
Bake for about 25–35 minutes or until the bread is baked through.

To check if the bread is baked, take a loaf out of the oven, tip it upside
down and tap it on the base. If it sounds hollow, the loaf is perfectly
baked. If it is not baked, replace the bread in the tin, place it back in the
oven and test again in a few minutes. Cool the loaf by removing it from
the tin and placing it on a wire rack.

baking with my father

CHEESE OMELETTE

SERVES 1

2 eggs, beaten

2 tablespoons water

Salt and pepper

A knob of butter

30g grated Cheddar cheese

Peter's fluffy cheese omelette was another popular lunchtime choice, made in an ancient copper pan handed down over the generations. When Dad showed me how to make this omelette I realized that he must have made thousands in his lifetime. My son, Joe, is now a big fan of these omelettes.

Put the eggs in a basin and add the water, gently whisking the mixture with a fork. Whisk in the salt and pepper.

Warm an omelette pan over a medium heat and, when it is hot, add the knob of butter. Pour in the egg mixture. Shake the pan to spread the mixture around the base evenly. Then take a large spoon or spatula and draw the omelette edges in towards the centre. Constantly move the mixture within the pan by both gently shaking the pan by the handle and turning the egg mixture with the spoon or spatula.

Once the mixture has thickened across the pan and is no longer liquid, reduce the heat and spread the cheese along the centre of the egg disc. Fold 1 side of the egg disc over the other to create a half-moon shape, then allow the cheese to warm through. Cook the omelette for about 30 seconds, gently shaking the pan to ensure it does not stick. Once cooked, turn out the omelette onto a plate and serve.

baker's tip

Do not overbeat the egg by using a whisk.
A fork is sufficient to add a little bit of air to
the mixture and ensure a smooth consistency.

baking with my father

QUICHE

Quiche was on the lunchtime menu and was sold over the counter. It was served with good old fashioned Heinz baked beans in the winter months or salad in the summer. Mum made her first quiche at the age of seventy five, which just goes to show you are never too old to start baking.

SERVES 8-10

FOR THE SHORTCRUST PASTRY (MAKES 225g)

225g plain flour, plus extra for dusting
½ teaspoon salt
100g butter, plus extra for greasing
2 tablespoons cold water

FOR THE FILLING

2 medium eggs, beaten
135ml single cream
135ml milk
A pinch of cayenne pepper
½ teaspoon salt
50g Cheddar cheese, grated
1 medium tomato, sliced

Sift the flour and salt into a bowl, then rub in the butter until the mixture resembles fine breadcrumbs. Add just enough cold water to allow the mixture to come together into a stiff dough, pressing it together with your fingertips. Wrap the dough in cling film and leave it to rest in the refrigerator for 30 minutes.

Grease a 20cm flan tin that is 3cm deep. Roll out the dough so that it is a little larger than the flan tin. Ease the pastry into the tin and trim any overhanging pastry. Stab holes into the base of the dough with a fork and rest it once again in the refrigerator for 15 minutes. Preheat oven to 170ºC/gas mark 3.

Line the flan tin with baking parchment and pour in some baking beans. Bake the dough for 15 minutes, then carefully remove the ceramic beans and parchment and bake for a further 5 minutes or until just golden.

Meanwhile, put the eggs into a mixing bowl and mix in the cream, milk, cayenne, salt and grated cheese. Pour the mixture into the flan case and arrange the sliced tomato on top. Bake for 30–40 minutes or until the egg mixture has set, when it should puff up nicely.

baker's tip

Instead of tomatoes use 25–50g chopped ham or 2 tablespoons chopped mushrooms. Use cream instead of milk to make a richer mix.

WELSH RAREBIT

SERVES 4 AS A SNACK

4 tablespoons milk

4 medium eggs

Salt and freshly ground black pepper,
 to taste

250g grated mature Cheddar cheese

1 teaspoon English mustard

4 thick slices of white bread

Welsh rarebit was the number one lunch choice. This was a 'secret recipe' so when Dad showed me how to make the Welsh in his retirement I felt honoured that I'd finally been let into the secret. In the tea shop we also served the Welsh with a poached egg on top, which was known as a buck rarebit.

Using a fork, mix the milk and eggs together, add some seasoning, then stir the mixture into the cheese. Once mixed, add the mustard and continue to stir.

Preheat the grill on a medium setting. Place the bread on a baking sheet and toast it on both sides. Now completely cover one side with the mixture to a depth of at least 5mm. Grill the topped toast until the cheese is bubbling and golden brown.

baker's tip

The Welsh rarebit mixture is always best left overnight and used the following day. If you do this, ensure you give it a good stir before topping the toast with it. Add roughly 1 tablespoon Lea & Perrins Worcestershire sauce to the cheese mixture to give the Welsh rarebit that extra bite. You can add 2 tablespoons chopped-up ham or bacon to the cheese mixture. You could also add some thin slices of tomato on top before cooking.

baking with my father

chapter eight

The Baker's Hands
Comfort Cakes

When Dad became housebound in 2012 he was given Holy Communion regularly at home by Father Jude – the priest who had married my parents. At first, he refused to have the anointment of the sick, afraid, I think, that it may have signified that he was dying. Dad was stubborn and hated being sick. He'd only closed the shop once due to sickness in forty two years.

A few days before one of his visits, Father Jude had phoned me up out of the blue to ask how Dad was feeling. Father Jude explained that a friend had called, telling him of Peter's declining health. I hadn't spoken to Father Jude for years and blurted out my feelings to the poor priest. "He's got no energy, he spends most of the time in bed. He's had a chest infection since Christmas and hasn't recovered; he's having blood tests and regular transfusions. He wobbles when he walks, I'm worried he's going to fall over, he's very down. He can't get out of the bath."

In the preceding weeks, Johnny had taken to visiting the family home in the early evening to yank his seventy-nine-year-old father out of the bath. Peter was a big man, far too heavy for Frankie to lift. On one occasion that Johnny attempted to do this, he said, "I nearly fell in the bath and landed on him!"

"It's depressing," I admitted to Father Jude. "When I go round he's either in bed or just sits on the sofa and holds my hand." I didn't use the word 'depressing' lightly. Lately I'd had this heavy feeling as I walked down the lane to visit Dad. I wanted him to be in the kitchen baking again but I knew he would be in bed. "Holding hands is a sign he loves you," said Father Jude, snapping me out of my introspection. "He probably finds it too hard to talk. Holding hands is much easier." I welled up, holding back the tears on the phone to the Catholic priest. Father Jude was right. Dad struggled to breathe and was frustrated he had no energy. "How is your Mum?" This question hurt further, went straight to my heart.

"She does everything. Gives him his pills, his insulin injections, does all the shopping, cooks for him. She drives him to hospital."

"It's a sign of her love for your father," he said. "She wants to do everything and he likes her being there."

I take a deep breath. "Yes."

And so it had come to this, that my father, the once-strong baker, was weakened by failing blood cells and bone marrow and who knew what else. My mother's life revolved around taking him to the doctor and the hospital for check ups, tests and blood transfusions. Dad was lucky he had married a nurse.

PETER STOPPED BAKING when his illness worsened. At our last masterclass, Mum and I made a ginger cake while Dad sat on the stool giving instructions. The baker's wife was by now a very good baker.

Mum had made her traditional ginger cake for Father Jude and gave me a slice on a visit home. "Cup of tea and some cake?" she asked.

"Yes please. Sorry I'm late. Lara was playing hockey so I had to drop her off en-route."

"Your father's in bed. He waited up, but I sent him back when he got tired."

Mum handed me a cup of tea and a slice of ginger cake. There was something about the simple combination of tea and homemade cake that comforted me. Mum's ginger cake had become her signature sponge, which she made for Dad, family and friends. Although Dad couldn't bake any longer, Mum continued the tradition without any need for discussion, simply ensuring there was a constant supply of freshly baked pastries. Until Dad's illness, she had never had reason to bake her own cakes. But when Dad stopped baking she was suddenly there in the kitchen, at the age of seventy five, making all the classic cakes: lemon drizzle, coffee and walnut, carrot, chocolate banana loaf.

Mum busied herself in the kitchen, whizzing up potato and leek soup with Joe, who had come with me. I had stopped asking if Dad might be fit enough to bake with me again.

I reflected on our baking sessions – both of us with our aprons on, Dad teaching me the old-fashioned tricks of the trade, Mum watching, sometimes dashing out for last-minute ingredients, always sharing memories of the tea shops. Over the last few years, we'd made most of the favourite cakes and pastries Dad had made when in his prime. But it wasn't just

the cake making and baking, the sweet scents and tastes, that reminded me of my childhood. It was always far more than just about cake.

It is only now that I realize why it took me until my forties to spend precious time with Dad in the kitchen. I had always taken for granted that Dad made cakes for every special occasion in the same way that I assumed Dad would always be there. This cake-making odyssey gave me special time with Dad before he became ill. If I had learned to bake earlier and become a pastry chef we'd never have spent all those months and years baking, chatting about cakes and tea shops and enjoying other father–daughter conversations. Now, my memories span my childhood in a tea shop and learning as a mother both to bake fairly late in life and enjoy the company of my baker father and family.

After my tea and cake, I tiptoed upstairs and popped my head around Dad's bedroom door. The room was dark, the curtains drawn. I could hear the sound of gentle breathing. "Is that you, darling?"

"Sorry, I didn't want to wake you."

"It's ok. Come here." He looked startled.

"Don't get up," I whispered. "Try to dream about our holidays in Ireland."

"Yes," he closed his eyes.

We always went for long walks in and around Avoca, up 'The hill with the cross', as we called it. Dad strode ahead of us, a strong man full of energy, us kids lagging behind, looking out for leprechaun bones. Dad always took the boys camping and fishing and we all went walking across the Wicklow Mountains, around rock pools and along streams. He once jumped into the water to save me when I lost my step and fell in.

Dad attempted a smile and we held hands; the hands that baked and made the many thousands of loaves and cakes.

IN THIS CHAPTER are recipes for cakes that are comforting and that will soothe you and lift your spirits. They are classic, unfussy cakes, reliable and uplifting, just like a loyal friend.

FRANKIE'S LEMON DRIZZLE CAKE

SERVES 8–10

175g margarine, plus extra for greasing

175g caster sugar, plus extra for sprinkling

Juice and grated zest of 2 lemons

2 large eggs, beaten

175g self-raising flour

1 teaspoon lemon extract

2 tablespoons milk

2 tablespoons granulated sugar

Dad occasionally made a lemon loaf cake in the shop. After he and Mum retired in 2000, they redid the kitchen at home and got a new oven. Mum was finally given the freedom to bake. At first, Dad continued to make big batches of cakes, but this lemon drizzle cake swiftly became Mum's signature cake, because she particularly liked it, and so did everyone else!

Preheat the oven to 180°C/gas mark 4. Grease a 900g loaf tin and line it with baking parchment.

Cream the margarine and sugar together with the zest of 1–1½ lemons. Mix in the beaten egg gradually, alternating these additions with tablespoons of the flour. Blend in the lemon extract and milk. Spoon the batter into the prepared loaf tin and smooth the surface with a palette knife. Bake for 40–50 minutes or until a skewer inserted into the centre of the cake comes out clean.

Towards the end of the cooking time, heat the lemon juice, granulated sugar and remaining lemon zest in a pan for 5 minutes until syrupy. When the cake is baked, while it is still hot from the oven, pierce many tiny holes in the cake using a skewer, pushing it roughly three-quarters of the way from the top surface into the cake. Drizzle some of the lemon mix into each hole, then spoon the remaining lemon mixture over the top surface. Sprinkle a little caster sugar on the top. Leave the cake in the tin for 10 minutes to allow the lemon mixture to soak into the sponge, then turn out the cake and leave on a wire rack until it is completely cool.

baker's tip

Paper loaf cases, available in specialist kitchen shops and good supermarkets, do away with the need to grease and line a tin; they give your loaf cakes a professional appearance – which is particularly good if you want to present one as a gift (lemon drizzle is a favourite for many).

the baker's hands

CARROT CAKE

SERVES 8-10

225g carrots, peeled and grated

3 eggs, beaten

175g self-raising flour

350g caster sugar

100ml olive oil

When carrot cake became popular we attempted to persuade Dad to make it in the shop. Dad was a traditionalist who stuck with the old-fashioned cakes, but after several years he made the carrot cake, much to everyone's surprise. When Dad retired he made carrot cake with my son Joe who added some icing on top. Dad couldn't resist making some marzipan carrot shapes to decorate it with.

Preheat the oven to 180°C/gas mark 4. Grease a 20cm round cake tin that is 7cm deep and line it with baking parchment.

Put the carrots into a large bowl and pour over the beaten eggs. Sift the flour and sugar into the bowl, then drizzle in the olive oil. Mix all the ingredients together well.

Pour the mixture into the prepared baking tin and bake for 35–50 minutes or until a skewer inserted into the centre of the cake comes out clean. Allow the cake to cool in the tin for about 5 minutes, then turn it out onto a wire rack.

baker's tip

Grind the carrots to the texture you require in a food processor. Dad made marzipan carrot shapes to decorate the top of the cake. Use the marzipan fruits recipe (see page 126) for guidance and simply shape the orange marzipan into a carrot shape. Dad didn't ice the cake, but you can ice it according to your taste. I recommend the following recipe: using a spatula or a wooden spoon, mix 250g full-fat cream cheese and 250ml double cream with 1 tablespoon caster sugar. Spread the mixture onto the cake with a palette knife. You don't need to add any more flavours.

COFFEE AND WALNUT CAKE

SERVES 10

225g butter, softened, plus extra for greasing

225g caster sugar

About 4 eggs (you need 225g)

4 tablespoons Camp Coffee Essence (or 2 tablespoons instant coffee dissolved in 4 tablespoons warm single cream)

250g self-raising flour

115g walnuts, roughly chopped, plus 8–10 walnut halves, to decorate

FOR THE COFFEE BUTTERCREAM

120g butter, softened

120g icing sugar

½ tablespoon Camp Coffee Essence (or 1 teaspoon instant coffee dissolved in 1 tablespoon warm single cream)

For more than forty years Dad made coffee and walnut cake every week and it was the cake he requested for his eightieth birthday celebration. His love of this cake goes back to when he was a boarder at St George's College, Weybridge, and was taken for tea by his parents to *Fuller's* tea room in Weybridge, where he later set up *Peter's*. Even today, there remains a *Fuller's* inscription on the tiled step entrance to the former tea shop.

Preheat the oven to 180°C/gas mark 4. Grease 2 x 20cm round sandwich tins and line the bases with baking parchment.

Using handheld electric beaters or a freestanding food mixer, cream the butter and sugar together for 2–3 minutes until the mixture is pale and fluffy.

Using a fork, beat the eggs with the coffee essence in a jug. Gradually beat this into the creamed butter and sugar. Fold in the flour until you have a smooth batter, then gently fold the chopped walnuts through the mixture, ensuring they are evenly distributed.

Divide the mixture between the prepared tins. Bake for 20–25 minutes until a skewer inserted into the centre of the cakes comes out clean. Leave the cakes to cool in the tins for 5 minutes, then transfer them to a wire rack to cool completely.

To make the buttercream, put the butter, icing sugar and coffee essence in a bowl and beat them together for 3–4 minutes until the mixture is light and fluffy.

To assemble the cake, place 1 sponge on a plate or cake stand and cover the top with about half of the buttercream, then position the other sponge on top. Cover the top surface with the remaining buttercream, smoothing it with a palette knife. Decorate the top of the cake with the walnut halves to finish.

baker's tip
Alternate halved glacé cherries with the halved walnuts on the top of the cake to add a pretty splash of colour.

CHOCOLATE-TOPPED FRESH CREAM SPONGE

SERVES 8-10

Butter, for greasing

100g caster sugar

Approximately 3 eggs (you need 160g), beaten

100g plain flour

1 teaspoon vanilla essence

FOR THE FILLING AND TOPPING

80g dark chocolate, broken into pieces

300ml whipping cream

2 teaspoons caster sugar (optional)

2 tablespoons seedless raspberry or smooth plum jam (optional)

Dad made this sponge cake on Saturdays only, as it was considered a family treat for the weekends. The light vanilla sponge with a chocolate coating is best eaten on the day it's made, which isn't too hard a challenge.

Preheat the oven to 180°C/gas mark 4. Grease a 20cm round cake tin that is 7cm deep and line it with baking parchment.

Whisk the sugar and egg together for about 10 minutes until the mixture is light and fluffy. Sift the flour onto the creamed mixture and very gently fold it in. Mix in the vanilla essence.

Spoon the mixture into the prepared tin and bake for about 20 minutes until the sponge is golden brown and begins to come away from the sides of the cake tin. Tip out the sponge, with the flat base facing up, onto a wire rack and leave it to cool completely.

Melt the chocolate in a bowl set over a pan of simmering water. Spread the melted chocolate thinly over the sponge. Set it aside to allow the chocolate to cool. Once the chocolate topping has set, cut the sponge horizontally to create 2 sponge layers. Then, using a warmed sharp knife, cut the layer of chocolate-topped sponge into 6 portions.

Whip the cream until it is thick, adding the caster sugar as you whip if you prefer a slightly sweeter cream.

Spread the jam onto the top surface of the bottom layer of sponge. Top this with a layer of whipped cream, then place the portioned chocolate-topped slices on top of the cream. Chill the cake until you are ready to serve.

baker's tip

If you are a big fan of chocolate, you can apply a second layer of melted chocolate over the first, once the first has set before cutting the sponge layer into portions. You might like to decoratively mark this layer with a combed scraper or the back of a fork before the chocolate sets.

CHOCOLATE BANANA LOAF

MAKES 1

100g dark chocolate (with 70 per cent cocoa solids)

110g margarine, plus extra for greasing

125g caster sugar

2 eggs, beaten

125g self-raising flour

1½ tablespoons cocoa

1 level teaspoon baking powder

2 medium bananas, mashed

Dad occasionally made banana loaf in the tea shop and Mum has added some chocolate to the mix. Not surprisingly, children love this cake. It can be transformed into a pudding if it is heated and served with cream or ice cream.

Preheat the oven to 180°C/gas mark 4. Grease a 900g loaf tin and line it with baking parchment.

Melt the chocolate in a bowl set over a pan of simmering water. Using a handheld whisk, cream the margarine with the sugar. Gradually add the eggs, beating the mixture constantly.

Meanwhile, sift the flour, cocoa and baking powder and add them to the mixture. Mix the mashed bananas in to the mixture with the melted chocolate, stirring well with a wooden spoon.

Pour the batter into the prepared cake tin. Bake for 40–50 minutes or until a skewer inserted into the centre of the cake comes out clean. Allow the cake to cool in the tin for 10 minutes, then turn it out onto a wire rack to cool completely.

baker's tip

It's best to use ripe bananas for this recipe because they mash easily into the mixture. If you want to decorate this cake, drizzle melted chocolate over the top or lay on sliced dried bananas once the cake has cooled.

APPLE CAKE

SERVES 8-10

110g caster sugar, plus extra for sprinkling

110g margarine, plus extra for greasing

1 egg

225g self-raising flour

A pinch of salt

4 tablespoons milk

Approximately 1 large Bramley apple (you need 225g), peeled, cored and cut into small pieces

Growing up in a tea shop meant that as adults we contributed to ingredients if we found anything Dad could use. My sister lived near a farm and occasionally purchased sacks of windfall apples at just two pounds each. One of Mum's favourite cakes is this moist sponge with pieces of apple. Nothing offers comfort quite like apple pie or cake.

Preheat the oven to 180°C/gas mark 4. Grease a 15cm round cake tin that is 7cm deep and line it with baking parchment.

Beat the sugar and margarine with a handheld whisk until the mixture is light and fluffy. Then beat in the egg. Add the flour, salt, milk and apples and mix them in well.

Pour the batter into the prepared tin and smooth the top with a palette knife. Bake for about 1 hour until the cake is golden and springy and a skewer inserted into the centre comes out clean. Sprinkle caster sugar over the cake while it is still hot. Leave the cake to cool in the tin for about 5 minutes, then turn it out onto the wire rack.

baker's tip

This cake is best eaten within 2 days because, due to its fruit content, it won't keep any longer. However, it rarely lasts that long in our house.

GINGER AND DATE CAKE

SERVES 10

110g butter, plus extra for greasing

110g light brown muscovado sugar

150g golden syrup

275g plain flour

1 teaspoon ground ginger

½ teaspoon salt

½ teaspoon bicarbonate of soda

½ teaspoon baking powder

100g dates, roughly chopped

1 large egg

175ml milk

This is a classic combination of two of Dad's favourite ingredients: ginger and dates. I made it one summer's day and the family all enjoyed tea and cake in Johnny's pretty garden overlooking the vineyard where Dad helped to trim the vines in his retirement. He even drove a tractor there on several occasions, which he loved, like a big kid.

Preheat oven to 160°C/gas mark 3. Grease a 20cm round cake tin that's approximately 7cm deep and line it with baking parchment.

Melt the butter, sugar and syrup in a saucepan. Sift the flour, ground ginger, salt, bicarbonate of soda and baking powder into a large bowl. Toss in the chopped dates and mix everything together. Stir in the melted butter mixture lightly, then follow by mixing in the egg and milk until all is thoroughly combined.

Pour the batter into the prepared cake tin and bake for 45–50 minutes. After 20 minutes, cover the top of the cake loosely with a circle of baking parchment to ensure it doesn't burn on top. Leave the cake to cool in the tin for about 5 minutes, then turn out onto a wire rack to cool completely.

baker's tip

If you would like to decorate this cake with ginger icing, make icing in the usual way by mixing 200g icing sugar plus approximately 2 tablespoons water and add 2–3 chopped slivers of stem ginger with 1 teaspoon syrup from the stem ginger jar.

the baker's hands

HOT CROSS BUNS

Dad made hot cross buns just at Easter, not all year round. Customers ordered them in advance because they went so quickly. The secret of their success was in Dad's glaze, which he made out of a sugar syrup flavoured with spices.

MAKES 12

30g fresh yeast or 14g fast-action dried yeast

50g caster sugar

200ml warm water

450g strong white bread flour, plus extra for dusting

40g milk powder

1 teaspoon salt

1 heaped teaspoon mixed spice

50g butter, melted and cooled

1 egg, beaten

75g currants

30g sultanas

50g mixed peel

Vegetable oil, for greasing

FOR THE SPICED BUN GLAZE

100g granulated sugar

4 crushed cardamom pods

4 cloves

1 teaspoon mixed spice

1 teaspoon grated nutmeg

1 teaspoon ground cinnamon

½ teaspoon allspice

100g water

FOR THE CROSS MIX

55g plain flour

15g vegetable oil

80g water

Put the yeast and 5g of the sugar into the warm water and set aside for about 10 minutes to ferment.

Mix the flour, milk powder, salt, mixed spice and remaining sugar together in a bowl. When the yeast is ready, add it to the flour mixture with the melted butter and beaten egg. Mix the ingredients together to a soft dough, then mix in the fruit and peel.

Knead the bun dough on a floured surface for about 10 minutes until it is smooth and elastic. Then put it in a lightly oiled bowl, cover the bowl with oiled cling film and leave it somewhere warm for 1–1½ hours until the dough has doubled in size.

Meanwhile, prepare the cross mix and bun glaze. To make the bun glaze, put the sugar and spices into a pan with the water and boil the mixture for 5 minutes. Then pass it through a sieve to remove the cardamom pods and cloves.

To make the cross mix, put the flour and oil in a bowl, then add the water gradually until the mixture has a good consistency for piping. Leave it to stand for a few minutes before use.

Grease a baking sheet with vegetable oil. Divide the risen dough into 12 pieces. Roll each piece between your hands into a smooth ball. Place these on the prepared baking sheet, spacing them about 3cm apart. Score a cross into the top of each bun. Leave the dough in a warm place to prove for about 40–60 minutes.

Preheat the oven to 200°C/gas mark 6.

Put the cross mix into a piping bag fitted with a small, round nozzle and pipe crosses onto buns over the scored crosses. Bake for 15–20 minutes until the buns are golden brown. Allow the buns to cool slightly on the baking sheet for 5 minutes, then brush each of them with the warm bun glaze. Allow the glaze to set before serving them with or without butter or toasted. They are best served fresh on the day they are baked, and are perfect without any additions. Toast the next day with a generous dollop of butter.

baker's tip

Do not be tempted to put too much spice in the bun dough as this can 'kill' the yeast – that is why a spiced bun glaze is used. Feel free to experiment with types and quantities of spices to discover what suits you.

SHORTBREAD

SERVES 12

85g butter, softened

55g caster sugar, plus extra for dusting
and sprinkling

85g plain flour

30g semolina

Shortbread is the classic afternoon biscuit, served with a pot of tea. The tea shop attracted elderly folk who spent afternoons putting the world to rights while sipping tea and devouring biscuits and cakes. The shortbread Dad made was thick, with a crinkle-cut edge and sprinkled with sugar. People rarely dunked biscuits in their tea in *Peter's* but this is the perfect dunking biscuit.

Preheat the oven to 130°C/gas mark ¾. Line a baking sheet with some baking parchment.

Cream the butter and sugar together in a bowl using a wooden spoon. Mix in the flour and semolina. Use your hands to mould the mix into the shape of a ball.

Dust the work surface with caster sugar. Roll out the dough lightly until it is about 1cm thick. Use a 6–7cm round cutter (fluted, if possible) to cut the biscuit shapes. Arrange the shapes on the prepared baking sheet. Bake for 25–30 minutes or until the shortbread looks pale golden. Leave the biscuits to cool on a wire rack, and sprinkle over some caster sugar while they are still warm.

baker's tip

For the authentic look, use a fork to perforate
the dough before cutting out the biscuits.
Store in an airtight tin for up to 3 days.

the baker's hands

chapter nine

Poschiavo and Pastry Chefs
European Pastries

From the moment I first read about Poschiavo, a village on the Swiss–Italian border, in the book of family history written by my relative Bernadette Forer, I longed to go in search of my heritage. I learned from this book that our ancestors came from Poschiavo, where there was an 'overabundance' of pastry chefs. Could this explain why so many of our forebears became bakers and why they emigrated?

I spent many hours talking to Dad about our family history, jogging him for any memories. He had never visited Poschiavo, but together we traced the family line down his mother's side. This is what we discovered: my great-great grandfather, Carlo Bernardo Forer, was one of a set of twins, born in Poschiavo in September 1839. Carlo married Maria Beti on June 20, 1870, in Poschiavo. They had six children, including Ferdinando, my great-grandfather, born in Marseille in 1877. On November 3, 1897, Ferdinando married Angelina Luminati (born in Poschiavo, January 3, 1878) and they had five children, including my grandmother, Leonylda (Dad's mother) and Uncle Charlie, who taught Dad how to make chocolates. Dad showed me some classic old family photographs of my grandmother and her siblings, plus some of my grandparents on their wedding day.

There was only so much researching, writing and baking I could do. I simply had to go to Poschiavo. I made email contact with Bernadette in Canada, who suggested I try to find a woman called Ida Luminati – with such a wonderful name, how could I resist? Ida is the daughter of Aristidie and Teresina Luminati. Aristidie was a pastry chef who ran the *Bernina Café* in Poschiavo and Angelina, my great-grandmother, was his sister. The pastry chef plot thickened. Dad told me that the Japonaise cakes he had made in *Peter's* had their roots in Poschiavo. Coffee Japs, as we called them, are almond meringue biscuits filled with coffee buttercream. Dad also made vanilla and chocolate Japs. Since the shop closed in 2000, I had not set eyes on a single one. I may have been travelling in search of my heritage, but I was also looking for a decent Jap.

Armed with the family book, I flew to Zurich and drove to Poschiavo; the sky was bright blue, on either side of the road were lush manicured fields, traditional wooden Swiss chalets and farms. After the Julier Pass came the Bernina Pass – endless tunnels, Alpine mountains and hairpin bends. The Poschiavo Valley used to be cut off during the harsh winters; now I understood why my ancestors were forced to escape this remote place.

After a three and a half hour journey I reached Poschiavo, excited and relieved. I discovered most people spoke Italian but also understood English. At my hotel, I showed the female owner my family book and she shared it with her father who remembered Aristidie Luminati and the *Bernina Café*. She told me Aristidie was nicknamed Churchill because of his resemblance to the former British Prime Minister. Locals called his business *Churchill's Café*. On learning this, I felt as if I had made a connection with my past.

Poschiavo reminded me of the small French village in Joanne Harris's novel, *Chocolat*, dominated by the church and the chocolate shop. The heart of Poschiavo is the piazza where people while away the day sipping cappuccinos. Down every little cobbled lane I spotted a café or restaurant. On the edge of the piazza lay the town's Catholic church, Parrocchia Cattolica Vittore Mauro, with a Roman bell tower. Every half hour, even through the night, the bell rang.

I assumed that in such a small village the best place to enquire about Ida was at one of the cafés on the piazza. I ordered a cappuccino and asked the waiter if he knew who Ida was and where she lived. After much gesticulation and some fiery sounding Italian exchanges, an older man called Franco drew a little map to her apartment. I walked a few hundred yards and went up to the wooden door where I saw Ida Luminati's name by a buzzer. I stood there stunned. Until then, Ida had just been a name to me. I pressed the bell and waited. I heard a door creak open and someone speak in Italian. I walked into the large main hall and peered up the stairs to see a lady in her eighties standing at a door, wearing glasses, with an apron tied around her waist. I walked up the stairs, said "*Ciao*", and tried to explain who I was.

She didn't understand English and kept shaking her head in confusion, uttering Italian words. Despite our communication issues she invited me into her home. I opened the family book and pointed at some photographs. She stopped at a page showing her father, Aristidie, with my grandmother, Leonylda, in Paris. She then showed me a photograph in a frame of a young Aristidie wearing a white baker's outfit, posing by a magnificent cake. I asked if I could take a picture of her holding the image and she agreed. By now, we were managing to communicate. She told me that Aristidie had run *Café Bernina*, now called *Café Flora*. Ida showed me a tourist information brochure containing the photo of Aristidie with the cake. It

confirmed the family reputation as well-known pastry chefs in Poschiavo. As I left Ida's apartment I felt I had finally made a personal connection with my family's past.

During the rest of my stay I visited the local churches, the cemetery, Lake Poschiavo, the Forer family house and, of course, the cafés. In one tea shop I noticed the various confections bore a resemblance to cakes Dad made. There were lemon-iced biscuits called pasticceria secca, fruit tarts with cream on top and pastries dotted with berries. At the *Pasticceria Alpina* I spotted an almond macaroon similar to Dad's. It tasted familiar, too: crunchy on the outside and soft inside, with an almond paste centre. On my final morning I visited the *Tea Room Caffe and Pasticceria*. I walked up to the counter and was rooted to the spot by what I saw: a tray of coffee Japs. I ordered one to eat in the café and one to take home for Mum and Dad. I took a bite of the crunchy almond biscuit and the soft coffee cream. This was definitely the closest I had come to tasting the cake Dad had made. All of a sudden I was back in the bakehouse, flour all over my school uniform, safe at home, surrounded by my family and cakes, watching Dad roll the Japs in the almond-biscuit mixture.

WHEN I RETURNED FROM POSCHIAVO, I asked Dad if he'd give a coffee Japonaise masterclass. He obliged and we invited my friend Karen and Johnny. Dad taught us how to make the almond meringue biscuits and the buttercream filling and showed us the decorating techniques. At each stage I learned something new, such as how to pipe the meringue mixture, or how to fill and decorate the biscuits. It was a remarkable baking experience and, for once, when I saw the finished cakes, I was stuck for words.

The biscuits were golden, crunchy and infused with almond, the coffee buttercream filling tasted smooth and mellow, the dark chocolate on top added an extra cocoa sweetness. I had finally made the coffee Jap with Dad. I promised to share the recipe in my baking memoir and return to Poschiavo with Lara and Joe, the next generation of pastry chefs.

In this chapter I share the recipes for the coffee Jap and also for a selection of popular European pastries served in Poschiavo and made by Dad in *Peter's*.

BELGIAN BUNS

MAKES 8

10g dried yeast or 20g fresh yeast

40g caster sugar

125ml warm water

300g strong bread flour, plus extra for dusting

1 teaspoon salt

5g milk powder

Approximately 1 egg (you need 25g), beaten

40g butter, softened, plus extra for greasing

120g sultanas

FOR THE BUN GLAZE

2–3 tablespoons water

220g icing sugar

8 glacé cherries

In the days when there was a local bobby who walked the streets of Weybridge, he regularly popped in to visit Dad in the bakehouse. One policeman always enjoyed a Belgian bun or two with a mug of tea. The policeman's uniform always got coated in flour, which was a small price to pay for a sticky Belgian bun.

Put the yeast and 5g of the sugar into the warm water and leave the mixture to ferment for about 10 minutes.

Mix the flour, salt, milk powder and remaining sugar together in a large bowl. When the yeast is ready, add it to the flour mixture with the egg and softened butter. Mix the ingredients well to combine. If the dough seems too sticky, add an extra tablespoon of flour to the dough. Add the sultanas, then knead the dough for about 10 minutes until it is smooth.

Put the dough into a lightly oiled bowl and cover this with some oiled cling film. Put the bowl in a warm place and leave the dough to rise for 1½–2 hours or until it has doubled in size.

Grease a baking sheet and line it with baking parchment. On a floured surface, knock back the dough and divide it into 8 equal pieces. Roll each piece into a sausage shape that's about 16cm long. Tie each of these into a knot. Place these onto the baking sheet, spacing them 3cm apart. Cover the baking sheet loosely with oiled cling film and leave the dough in a warm place to prove until it has doubled in size, which will take 30–40 minutes.

Preheat the oven to 190°C/gas mark 5. Bake for 12–15 minutes until the buns are golden brown. Cool on the baking sheet for a few minutes, then transfer them to a wire rack.

Gradually add the water to the icing sugar, adding just enough water to get the right consistency – you want it to be thick enough to coat the back of a spoon. Apply the icing to the tops of the buns using a palette knife. Place a glacé cherry onto the middle of each bun.

baker's tip

If you like the flavour of almonds, it works very nicely with Belgian buns. Scatter some flaked almonds onto the tops of the knotted pieces of dough before you put them in the oven. You can then ice them in the usual way, or serve them without icing, depending on your preference.

JAM SWISS ROLL

SERVES 8–10

2 eggs

75g caster sugar, plus extra to sprinkle

75g self-raising flour

1 teaspoon baking powder

25g butter, softened

3–4 tablespoons smooth (seedless) raspberry jam

The Swiss roll may not have its origins in Switzerland but it's a popular European cake. Dad made various flavours: chocolate, vanilla and coffee. Swiss rolls form the basis for special cakes such as a Christmas log and the decadent chocolate roulade my sister makes with raspberries and cream.

Preheat the oven to 200°C/gas mark 6. Grease a 20 x 30cm Swiss roll tin and line it with baking parchment.

Whisk the eggs and sugar using an electric whisk until the mixture is light and fluffy.

Sift the flour and baking powder into the mixture. Fold this into the egg and sugar mixture, then add the butter. Continue to whisk for 1 minute to ensure the ingredients are well mixed.

Smooth the mixture into the prepared tin. Gently ease it into the corners of the tin using the back of a metal spoon. It may appear sparse but don't worry – it rises. Bake for 10–12 minutes until the sponge appears slightly golden and is springy. Meanwhile, cut a sheet of baking parchment that is a little larger than the tin and sprinkle over some caster sugar.

Remove the cake from the oven and leave it for 1 minute, then lift it out of the tin using the paper lining the tin. Tip the sponge gently onto the sugared paper with the top facing down. Peel off the liner carefully. Trim the sides of the cake with a sharp knife to make a neater rectangle. Place a clean damp tea towel over the cake for about 2 minutes – this will prevent cracking.

After the 2 minutes of waiting, spread the sponge with jam. Make a cut along the short edge of the cake about two-thirds of the way through the cake to help the rolling process. This allows the cake to gently bend. Roll carefully, holding the sugared paper behind the cake and pulling on it to make the roll move forwards. When the cake is rolled, hold the paper around the cake for a minute to set the shape. Transfer to a wire rack and sprinkle with caster sugar.

baker's tip

To make a coffee Swiss roll, add the following after folding in the flour: 2 tablespoons Camp Coffee Essence or 2 tablespoons instant coffee dissolved in 4 tablespoons water. For the buttercream, cream 50g butter with 75g icing sugar, add ½ teaspoon Camp Coffee Essence or 1 teaspoon instant coffee dissolved in 1 tablespoon water. Spread the mixture on the roll in place of the jam.

SWISS CREAM PASTRY HORNS

Vegetable oil, for greasing

210g puff pastry (see page 132 or use shop-bought)

30–55g caster sugar

170ml whipping cream

Approximately 2 tablespoons strawberry jam

Cream horns were one of the cream cakes traditionally served on the glass cake stand for afternoon tea. Fuby now has Dad's metal cornet moulds so, on occasions, she arrives at family gatherings with a plate of cream horns. They look so tempting with the cream oozing out. The baker's youngest daughter is a very talented baker.

Preheat the oven to 220°C/gas mark 7. Line 2 baking sheets with baking parchment. You'll need 10 cornet moulds for this recipe. Ensure you grease them well.

Roll out the pastry into a rectangle measuring 25 x 33cm. Working across the 25cm length, cut the pastry into 10 strips that are each 2.5cm wide. Dampen or moisten 1 long edge of 1 strip with water. Wind a strip of pastry around a cornet mould, starting at the point, ensuring you overlap the damp edge, until you have covered approximately one-third of the mould. Gently press the edges of the pastry together. Place the pastry and mould on a prepared baking sheet. Repeat with the remaining pastry strips and moulds. Place the baking sheets in the refrigerator for 15 minutes.

Dip each horn top in caster sugar, then replace it on the baking sheet. Bake for 15 minutes or until the pastry is golden. Wait for 5 minutes before carefully removing the pastry from the mould – it is easier to remove the pastry from the cornet mould while it is still slightly warm from the oven. Leave the pastries to cool on a wire rack until they are completely cold.

Whip the cream until stiff. Pipe or spoon a little jam into a horn pipe, then pipe in the cream. Repeat with the remaining pastries and fillings.

Poschiavo and pastry chefs

VIENNESE WHIRLS

MAKES 8

250g butter, softened

60g icing sugar

½ teaspoon vanilla extract

220g plain flour

75g cornflour

FOR THE FILLING

120g butter

170g icing sugar

Flavourings: 1 drop vanilla extract
for vanilla filling or 30g melted
chocolate or cocoa for chocolate
filling

4 tablespoons strawberry jam (for
vanilla filling)

If you like tea and biscuits, these traditional fancy whirls will be a treat.
They remind me of delicate shortbread, the perfect complement to a pot
of tea. Viennese whirls are also fun to make as you can experiment with
the fillings and decorations. Make them plain or pipe chocolate on top.

Preheat the oven to 180ºC/gas mark 4. Line a baking sheet with baking
parchment.

Beat the butter and icing sugar together with a wooden spoon, a handheld
electric whisk or a freestanding food mixer until the mixture is pale. Mix
in the vanilla extract. Sift in the flour and cornflour and beat the mixture
until it is smooth and the ingredients are well combined.

Put the mixture into a piping bag fitted with a large star nozzle. Pipe swirls
onto the prepared baking sheet that are approximately 6cm in size, starting
from the centre of the swirl and working in a spiral out to the edge of the
circle. Space these roughly 3cm apart.

Bake the swirls for 10–15 minutes until they are pale but not yet
browning. Place them on a wire rack to cool.

To make the filling, prepare the butter icing by beating together the butter
and icing sugar. Mix in the vanilla extract for vanilla-flavoured filling, or
the cocoa or melted chocolate for chocolate centres. Put the flavoured
butter icing into a piping bag fitted with a star nozzle. If you're using
vanilla filling, spread jam on a biscuit with a palette knife, keeping
it 1cm away from the edge of the biscuit. Now pipe butter icing on top,
again, keeping it 1cm from the edge. Use another biscuit to sandwich the
filling. If you're using chocolate butter icing, omit the jam and pipe the
mixture as described above. Repeat with the remaining biscuits.

baker's tip

For lemon-flavoured whirls,
use lemon curd instead of
jam and add 2–3 drops
of lemon extract.

Poschiavo and pastry chefs

CHOCOLATE VIENNESE FINGERS

MAKES 20

230g plain flour

30g cocoa

250g butter, softened

100g icing sugar

3 tablespoons egg whites
(approximately 2 egg whites),
lightly beaten

FOR THE FILLING AND DECORATION

75g butter

75g icing sugar

25g cocoa

150g dark chocolate, broken into pieces

These chocolate-flavoured finger biscuits are one of Gordon's favourites. The biscuit is a cross between chocolate-flavoured shortbread and Viennese whirls (see opposite). Both ends are dipped in pure chocolate. You don't see them very often so they are worth making, especially if you have a chocolate craving.

Preheat the oven to 160°C/gas mark 3. Line a baking sheet with some baking parchment.

Sift the flour and cocoa together. In another bowl, beat together the butter and icing sugar until the mixture is light in texture. Add the egg whites and beat the mixture until it is creamy. Fold in the flour and cocoa mixture.

Put the mixture into a piping bag fitted with a medium star nozzle and pipe 7cm lengths of the mixture onto the prepared baking sheet, spacing them 2.5cm apart. Bake for 15–20 minutes. Leave the biscuits to cool on a wire rack.

To make the filling, beat the butter with a wooden spoon until it is soft, then add the icing sugar and cocoa and beat the mixture well.

Spread the filling onto the base of half of the chocolate fingers. Now place the base of another finger on top and sandwich them together. Repeat with the remaining chocolate fingers.

Melt the chocolate in a bowl set over a pan of simmering water. When the chocolate has melted, take it off the heat and dip the end of each biscuit into the melted chocolate, dipping them about 2cm in. Place the dipped biscuits on a sheet of baking parchment to dry.

baker's tip

You can replace the chocolate buttercream centre with a thin layer of jam and vanilla buttercream in these finger biscuits.

COFFEE JAPONAISE

MAKES ABOUT 15

Approximately 8 egg whites (you
   need 140g)

225g caster sugar

1 teaspoon almond essence

110g ground almonds

Butter, for greasing

FOR THE COFFEE BUTTERCREAM FILLING

330g icing sugar

170g butter, softened

4 teaspoons coffee essence

25g dark chocolate containing
   70 per cent cocoa solids

This one cake conjures up so many memories. First, I picture Dad making these Japs in his prime in the bakehouse. I recall discovering a tray of coffee Japs in a tea shop in Poschiavo. Then Dad gave a masterclass in making Japs attended by Johnny and my friend, Karen, whose favourite cake is the coffee Jap. When I showed this recipe to the chef Albert Roux, he made me a vanilla-flavoured Japonaise, which is known as a success biscuit.

Preheat the oven to 150°C/gas mark 2. Grease 1 or 2 large baking sheets.

Whisk the egg whites to soft peaks. Add half the caster sugar slowly, spoonful by spoonful, then add the almond essence. Sift the ground almonds and remaining caster sugar into a second bowl and mix them together. Blend the dry ingredients into the meringue mixture.

Place the mixture into a piping bag with a 1cm plain nozzle and pipe about 35 spirals that are approximately 3–4cm in diameter (to make a 5cm biscuit – the mixture expands) onto the prepared baking sheet, spacing them about 3cm apart. Note that these biscuits are meant to be flat, like digestives. You can use a stencil or biscuit cutter to mark out the size on the tray prior to piping. Also, the mixture can be stencilled onto the tray using a rubber stencil (this was what my father did). Bake for approximately 20 minutes until the biscuits are golden brown. Leave them to cool on a wire rack.

baker's tip

It's easy to vary the flavour of the Japs. Peter made different varieties of Japonaise: coffee, vanilla and chocolate (all using the same biscuits). To make a chocolate Japonaise, fill the biscuits with chocolate buttercream, made using 1 tablespoon cocoa instead of coffee essence. Then dip the biscuits in melted dark chocolate. To make vanilla Japonaise, fill the biscuits with vanilla buttercream, made using 2 drops vanilla extract instead of the coffee essence. Dust these with sieved icing sugar.

Meanwhile, make the coffee buttercream filling. Sift the icing sugar into a bowl. Mix in the cubed butter to form a smooth paste. Now add the coffee essence.

Place 5 of the cooled biscuits in a plastic bag and crush them with a rolling pin to create Japonaise crumbs. Put these on a plate.

Pipe coffee buttercream onto half of the remaining biscuits with a clean piping bag fitted with a 1cm plain nozzle. Place the remaining biscuits upside down on the buttercream to create a sandwich, pressing down slightly to achieve uniform thickness of filling – you want the layer of buttercream to be 1–2cm thick. Using a palette knife, coat the sides of the biscuits with buttercream and roll each sandwich, like a wheel, in the Japonaise crumbs. Coat the tops with more buttercream and sift the Japonaise biscuit crumbs on top.

Melt the chocolate in a bowl set over a pan of simmering water. Spoon a dollop of melted chocolate onto the centre of each biscuit for decoration. Put the Japs on a tray and leave to one side until the chocolate has set.

Poschiavo and pastry chefs

LINZER BISCUITS

MAKES 24 BISCUITS *

400g plain flour, plus extra to dust
200g butter
200g caster sugar
2 eggs, or 1 egg and 1 yolk, beaten
¼ teaspoon salt
4 tablespoons seedless raspberry jam
Icing sugar, to dust

depending on the size of your cutter

I spotted Linzer biscuits in a café in Poschiavo and they looked just like the ones Dad made, with two biscuits sandwiched together, coated in icing sugar with a jam centre. At first, I was surprised to see them in this little Swiss–Italian village, but these are classic biscuits you'll see in many European cities.

Rub the flour and butter together until the mixture resembles fine breadcrumbs. Mix the sugar and beaten egg together in another bowl, then add this to the flour and butter mixture with the salt and mix until a dough is formed.

Wrap the dough in cling film and place it in the refrigerator for about 30 minutes. After this time, remove half of the dough, leaving the other half in the refrigerator to keep cool. Preheat the oven to 180°C/gas mark 4. Line a baking sheet with baking parchment.

Roll out the dough on a floured surface to a thickness of about 5mm. Using a 5.5cm round biscuit cutter, stamp out 24 circles and transfer these to the prepared baking sheet. Using a 2.5cm round cutter (or use different shapes, such as a star or a crescent), cut out shapes from the centres of half the circles.

Bake for about 8 minutes or until the biscuits are pale golden. Leave them on the baking sheet for 5 minutes to harden, then transfer them to a cooling rack. Spoon the jam evenly among the centres of the biscuits, leaving a border of the biscuit showing around the edges. Cover each jammed biscuit with a hole-cut biscuit, then dust the top with a little icing sugar. Repeat the process with the remaining dough if you want more Linzer biscuits, or freeze it for another occasion.

baker's tip
Using a fluted round biscuit cutter gives your biscuits a professional appearance.

Poschiavo and pastry chefs

ALMOND MACAROONS

MAKES 15

100g ground almonds
175g caster sugar
1 tablespoon ground rice
2 egg whites
Flaked almonds, to decorate

These were a traditional delicate cake enjoyed by civilized Weybridge folk. When Dad showed me how to make them I was surprised how simple the recipe was and how quickly they baked. I also saw almond macaroons in Poschiavo that looked and tasted very similar to Dad's, with an almond slice on top.

Preheat oven to 180°C/gas mark 4. Line a baking sheet with some baking parchment.

Mix the ground almonds, sugar and ground rice in a bowl, then beat in the egg whites. Place a ball of the mixture that's about the size of a small tomato onto the prepared baking sheet. Slightly flatten it to form a biscuit shape. Place 1 or a few flaked almonds on top for decoration. Repeat until all the mixture is used up.

Bake for 10–15 minutes until lightly cooked. Allow the macaroons to cool slightly on the baking sheet before transferring them to a cooling rack to cool completely.

baker's tip
Peter piped the mixture onto rice paper instead of baking parchment, but you can use a dessert spoon as it is roughly the quantity needed. You can also use the spoon to flatten the shape.

MINI MACARONS

MAKES APPROXIMATELY 20

175g icing sugar

150g ground almonds

3 large egg whites

25g caster sugar

2 drops pink food colouring – or the colour of your choice (you can add more drops to intensify the colour)

FOR THE FILLINGS

110g icing sugar

110g butter

An assortment of food flavours and colours, such as strawberry, lemon, pistachio – or the flavours of your choice

Mini macarons have become very popular in recent years. Lara and Mum now enjoy making them in different flavours and colours. They can be very expensive to buy so it's worth attempting to make your own. Both almond macaroons (see page 177) and mini macarons contain almonds, yet they are of completely different shapes and flavours.

Sift the icing sugar into a bowl, then stir in the ground almonds. Whisk the egg white until it is stiff using a handheld whisk. Add the caster sugar and continue to whisk until you have stiff peaks. Fold in the almond-and-icing sugar mixture. At this stage, the mixture can be divided and coloured, using food colourings to match any flavourings you might be using for the fillings. Put the macaron mixture into a piping bag fitted with a 2.5cm plain nozzle.

You can use a macaron mould to shape the mixture or draw circles that are approximately 2.5cm in diameter on a sheet of greaseproof paper, spacing them 2.5cm apart. Pipe the mixture onto the drawn circles or into the moulds on a large baking sheet. Tap the sheet on a table to level out the mixture. Set aside for 1½ hours, by which time a slight skin will have formed on the cakes.

Preheat the oven to 160°C/gas mark 3.

Bake for 12–15 minutes, then switch off the oven and leave the oven door slightly ajar until the macarons are firm. If you piped the mixture onto greaseproof paper, leave the macarons to cool on the paper.

To make the filling, mix the icing sugar and butter together until light and fluffy. Divide the mixture into portions, depending on the number of flavours/colours you would like to make, then add the colours and flavourings of your choice, starting with 1–2 drops and adding more if you think it is necessary. Place the mixture in a piping bag fitted with a 1cm plain nozzle. Pipe the filling onto half of a macaron, then place the other half of the macaron on top and sandwich them together around the filling.

baker's tip

If you are colouring the mini macaron mixture in different colours, prepare a separate piping bag for each colour, which will make the piping easier. Alternatively, use whipped cream or flavoured buttercream in place of the icing filling, if you prefer.

Poschiavo and pastry chefs

my baking journey

My journey into my baking history has always been about more than just baking. I started off writing stories about my family's tea shop, which led me to bake with my father and grow closer to him in the process. The baker's daughter discovered a lot about a baker's life and her pastry chef ancestors through baking. Besides, Dad was always most comfortable chatting about the tea shops in our family kitchen, with cakes in the oven. He revealed stories about relatives I knew nothing about, which sparked me to research our family tea shop tree and discover nine tea shops.

I went on an exciting journey to the Swiss–Italian town of Poschiavo, where I learned about the poverty and hardship that led to my ancestors emigrating to France and then branching out in England, making a living through running tea shops. I found the coffee Japonaise cake that Dad made in our tea shop in Weybridge in a little café in Poschiavo – evidence of our connection to this idyllic village in the scenic Alps. I transported one all the way back to Dad, who then gave a masterclass in making these European cakes that his family had taught him to make. The sight, scent and taste of the Japs made with Dad brought the tea shop alive for me again, which is what I have tried to do in this book through stories, recipes, and memories of customers, friends and family. I decided to do a PhD, which became my book-length baking memoir, with recipes featuring more extended tales from the tea shops.

The challenge of recreating the tea shop recipes was enormous for me. Dad's huge quantities and old-fashioned ingredients meant I had a lot of figuring out to do. Luckily, I wasn't on my own. Dad was by my side at the start of the journey, patiently putting up with my constant questions about tea shops and cakes until, one day, he virtually told me to stop questioning and start baking. The scent and taste of the different cakes brought back so many vivid memories of my childhood in the bakehouse that I soon realized this was the best way to write the book – through baking, listening and recording. We would start with a few ingredients, make a cake, share stories about the tea shops and write while the scent of the cakes still lingered in the air.

Sadly, Peter became ill during this magical process and so I unexpectedly had to accept his illness and decline. It was very hard to watch my once-strong baker father lose his strength and ability to bake. Looking back, by then he had handed me the baton, or the rolling pin, and it was down to me to continue what we had started together a few years earlier.

After Dad's death in April 2012, my family rallied around. Mum naturally took up the baking challenge with me along with my siblings and children. The first Christmas and Easter without Dad brought out all the bakers in the family. I made peppermint chocolates, Mum made the Christmas cake and marzipan fruits, Gordon made mince pies. In the past, Dad had made almost everything for us. At Easter, Mum made a simnel cake and delightful fondant fancies. Fuby baked English madeleines, cream horns and animal biscuits. Johnny created a perfect Parisian millefeuille. Lara made custard tarts, while Joe knocked out Scotch pancakes and shortbread. My siblings and I often bickered about baking, arguing about the important things in life, such as the best way to make éclairs and how to perfect macarons. We adapted Peter's old recipe cards and relied on our bakehouse memories. We all missed him terribly, but I'm sure baking helped heal some of the pain we felt at his loss.

That Christmas, I recalled the advice he gave me as we had baked together, how he had encouraged me to be confident and use my instinct. I knew I had lacked confidence in the kitchen. I was petrified of pastry from the start. While Dad had made pastry effortlessly for over forty years, I simply couldn't imagine ever making a decent fruit pie or quiche, let alone puff pastry and millefeuille. Meanwhile, it soon became obvious that Mum was a talented baker, as she turned out cake after cake on a weekly basis. One day it was Swiss roll, the next day, iced walnut cake. At the age of seventy-seven, she had finally discovered a passion for baking. Clearly, being married to a baker for over fifty years meant she had never needed to bake before. Mum's baking time had arrived. The day she showed us her showstopper simnel cake, we knew she had entered into a different baking league. Peter would have been so proud of her. Our cakes rarely looked or tasted exactly like Dad's but, in the end, I came to the conclusion that this didn't matter.

WHEN YOU ARE A BAKER'S DAUGHTER it's hard for any cakes to match your father's high standards and cakes in cafés and shops so often disappoint. My sister admits she is a terrible cake snob. However, this journey was always about more han just finding or creating perfect cakes. Making and writing about pastries helped to bring the tea shop traditions and stories alive again, and we are now creating a new future with the skills my father taught us. Lara and Joe are the next generation who love to bake.

I now have a few ancient recipe books from our other family tea shops that I'm looking at. The quantities, ingredients and measurements blow my mind, but I am curious about these cakes and pastry chef ancestors, their wartime sponges and strange-sounding ingredients. For me, cakes unlock stories and sometimes even mysteries unfold.

Dad's pink cottage cake will always be my favourite childhood birthday cake, as much for the pretty pink cake with its chocolate thatched roof as for the memories associated with parties in the tea room. There was also a unique baking experience during the writing of this book, when we made the cottage cake for my niece Hannah's eighteenth birthday. The cake took more than an afternoon to bake and decorate under Dad's guidance. This wasn't the first time I had wondered how Dad had made so many speciality cakes on top of the regular cakes, breads and chocolates he made every day in such a calm, understated manner for over forty years.

If there is one special small cake I'd like to share with readers, it has to be the coffee Japonaise. I have a black-and-white photograph of Dad in the bakehouse, taken in the 1960s, making the Japs. He looks strong and focused, baking in his prime. The Japs are hard to find these days. In the same way, it is also rare to find bakers like my father who devoted a lifetime to cakes.

I hope these stories and recipes from our family tea shop will inspire you to bake.

notes on ingredients

Below you will find some background information on the ingredients used by Peter, some stories about the use of these at *Peter*'s and the ingredients for baking that are recommended today.

EGGS Peter always used Imperial liquid measures of egg rather than numbers. I suppose it wouldn't have been realistic to expect to count fifty-plus eggs individually as he broke them into a mixing bowl. In writing the recipes, I've continued this tradition of measuring eggs by volume rather than number (opting for metric units of measurement for a modern audience), but I've also given approximate numbers of eggs when I feel it would be helpful (based on medium-sized eggs).

Peter had tens of dozens of eggs delivered by 'Frank The Egg' on a weekly basis. The cardboard boxes contained at least twenty trays of eggs each – a delivery you did not want to drop. This was before the days of organic produce, but I recall that they looked pretty organic. I remember the buckets of empty eggshells that were collected by the local pig farmer along with other appropriate food-waste items for 'swill'. Old eggshells had a purpose at home, too. Dad used to keep and breed canaries – the only hobby he had outside of his ninety-plus-hour weeks. Johnny remembers that Dad occasionally 'roasted' a tray of empty eggshells in the oven overnight and, the following day, he would finely crush them and feed them to the canaries as a valuable source of calcium. He even kept some canaries 'out the back' of the shop until the Environmental Health Officer intervened. Back home they went.

For best results with the recipes, I'd endorse the use of organic eggs. If you store your eggs in the refrigerator, ensure they are at room temperature before use.

FATS Peter used a range of fats for different purposes, all supplied by Crimony. When I was a child, these were delivered to him in twenty-eight-pound blocks

in cardboard boxes, but when he first opened the shop over fifty years ago, they were delivered in individual wooden crates that had to be opened with a claw hammer. To the day he closed the shop, he still used some of the wooden crates to store old baking tins.

One of the types of fat Dad used was cake margarine, which was exactly that: margarine designed for the baking of cakes. It predated the existence of spreading margarine as an alternative to butter. Modern-day margarine for baking cakes can be found in supermarkets and I suggest you do not use the spreadable option as an alternative because it is not the same thing.

I generally use unsalted butter unless otherwise stated in a recipe. If a recipe calls for softened butter, the butter should be removed from the refrigerator several hours before you intend to use it. If you forget, chop up the butter and leave it at room temperature for half an hour before use.

The Dundee cake calls for white vegetable fat rather than margarine. Again, this is relatively easy to source, but don't make the mistake of using lard in its place as this will end in disaster.

MILK Milk was always silver top and delivered in glass bottles by the crate on a daily basis. It was an easy delivery for the Dairy Crest milkman. He came in for a cup of tea and bun before most of the population had stirred in their beds.

I remember dozens of milk bottles were used daily in the shop and always left out for collection the following day. I can only imagine Dad's relief when the delivery changed to eight-pint plastic containers. In the recipes in this book I have used semi-skimmed milk unless otherwise stated. If you want a richer flavour, use full-fat milk.

CREAM The milkman also delivered the liquid cream for whipping. My father added a cupful of caster sugar to the cream after it had begun to thicken, but before it was whipped. Not only did this produce a particularly sweet cream, it also helped it retain its shape whilst on display in the shop. Fresh cream cakes did not remain for long before being purchased.

Clotted cream came from a supplier in the West Country and was delivered by post. For a number of years, Dad had personal deliveries of Jersey cream from a local farming family. He gave the milk maids doughnuts when they delivered this luxurious cream that made wonderful whipped cream.

FLOUR Flour was delivered in fifty-six-pound paper sacks made by Spillers. Prior to that, flour was delivered in hessian sacks. There were always two delivery drivers for Spillers. They took it in turns to bring the large sacks to the rear door, perfectly balanced on their shoulders, without the need to grip the sacks with their hands.

The vast majority of flour used in the shop was plain white flour and we got through at least half a ton per week. Other types included self-raising and grained flours for speciality breads. At one point Spillers

raised the size of the minimum delivery order, so Peter had to have a purpose-built brick outhouse constructed purely to store his flour.

Use standard plain flour unless otherwise stated. Organic options are available now but some produce a grainier texture in more delicate cakes and pastries.

SUGAR Sugar was supplied in centum weight (or hundredweight) bags, which were almost impossible to move until at least a third of the contents had been removed. Dad used to ladle the sugar out of the bags with an old metal saucepan without a handle. It probably held three pounds of sugar at a time and had been rubbed smooth over the years with countless scoops in and out of the sugar on a daily basis. The sugar of choice was Tate & Lyle.

Unless specified in the recipe, use caster sugar, which is commonly used in cake making as the small grains produce an even texture. Granulated, muscovado, brown sugars and molasses are used in some recipes. Granulated sugar has a coarser texture and is used in rubbed-in methods, such as that used for the palmiers.

Don't be fooled into thinking that demerara is the same as brown sugar, it is not. Demerara is white

In 1954, Dad (far left) was a member of the Southend-on-Sea Master Bakers Association, alongside his cousin John Forer (on his left) and my grandfather (under the Spillers sign). Dad worked in *Lane's* in Westcliff with his parents while John Forer worked with his family in *Beti's*, Southsea.

sugar that has been flavoured and coloured. To see the difference, put a dessertspoonful of demerara sugar into a glass with a small amount of cold water and swill gently. You will see that if you pour the water out carefully it will have discoloured to brown and the remaining sugar in the glass has become white. If you repeat this process with proper brown sugar, there is very little loss of colour.

JAM Jam came in metal tins, thirty pounds in weight, made by Renshaw (by Royal Appointment). It seems incredible to think that tin was used as a container considering the current cost of metals. Prior to tin, jam was delivered in brown earthenware jars with sealed tops. We still have some of these functional jars in the family. Johnny uses them to hold his cooking utensils.

Peter used various flavours of jam for different recipes, but in the majority, he used what was called 'confectionery jam'. This was a very plain, simple jam of no particular flavour. It was red, sticky, looked like jam and was extremely sweet. The most important factor was that it was smooth, without lumps of fruit, pips or seeds.

When it came to jam to serve with the scones, only the best full-fruit homemade strawberry jam would do. Dad sold his strawberry jam to some of the regular customers, but this soon expanded. Eventually, due to demand, he found himself regularly making vast quantities of the seasonal jam, which lined the shelves of the shop. In the winter months, Dad made three-fruit marmalade. Again, this eventually became produced in commercial quantities.

CHOCOLATE Apart from the Cadbury's Flakes we used for the pink cottage cake, only dark chocolate was used in the shop, whether as an ingredient in a recipe or as part of the decoration. Dark chocolate produces a much stronger flavour and has a higher melting point than milk chocolate, so it retains its texture and structure better.

For day-to-day decoration, or for the dipping of cakes, there was always a wok-shaped pan filled with molten chocolate that lived on top of the boiling water 'geezer' that provided hot water for the pots of tea. Dad used good-quality cooking chocolate that came in fourteen-pound boxes of chocolate buttons and the residual heat melted it quickly and easily. I used to love dipping a finger into the warm chocolate when no one was looking.

For the homemade chocolates, Peter used fine Belgian confectionery chocolate latterly produced by Callebaut, a specialist manufacturer. Unfortunately, Callebaut only supplied chocolate in large quantities to other manufacturers, but Peter negotiated a private arrangement as an independent user for a minimum of two hundred and fifty pounds at a time. Callebaut would not usually deliver such a paltry amount. Every couple of months we would take a family trip out to their distribution centre near Oxford and return with a boot-load of chocolate, heady from the sweet scent. It came in cardboard boxes that were about forty five pounds in weight. Inside, there were three individual 'slabs' of chocolate, each weighing fifteen pounds and looking just like a child's giant chocolate bar.

My grandfather always said that I had 'good hands' for becoming a confectioner, not because they were dainty, but because they were always cold. The single most important factor when dealing with chocolate is temperature and cold hands make success a lot easier to achieve. The chocolate must never be warmed directly over a heat source as it burns easily. It must never be boiled, or it will lose its shine. If it is not warm enough, it will either set within the piping bag, or set before it has been spread across a cake. Chocolate must be, like the baby bowl of Goldilocks porridge, 'just right'. Conversely, if you have to squeeze the piping bag to release the chocolate then it is too cool and too thick.

You are unlikely to be able to buy confectionery-quality chocolate 'off the shelf' if you are going to attempt to make homemade chocolates. However, for most of the recipes in this book, 70 per cent cocoa chocolate is fine and is available from all supermarkets.

ICING Various forms of icing were used in the shop, including the usual basic icing, royal icing and buttercream. Fondant icing was also used, again, supplied by Renshaw, and came in a twenty-eight-pound almost-solid block that had the consistency of putty and could only be removed from its container with a sharp knife and a lot of effort.

Fondant, or baker's fondant, as I have described it in this book, is not an easy product to buy in supermarkets. I am lucky enough to still have a 'friend' in the commercial baking world that can supply me with the genuine article. But I have seen packets of 'fondant icing sugar', which, upon examination, requires the user to just 'add water'.

Fondant is a great icing to use as it is simple to prepare, easy to store and is great at 'taking' a colour or flavour. It can be poured over cakes to produce a single uninterrupted coating of icing, without joints, or individual cakes can be dipped into fondant for a similar effect. It can also be piped and, as long as it is not overheated, it produces a reflective 'sheen' (almost a gloss) on the surface of the cake when it sets.

Renice was the Renshaw proprietary brand of ready-to-roll icing. It is available in most of the larger supermarkets and the modern-day version appears to be exactly the same as the product that Peter used. It comes in a plain white colour and has the consistency of plasticine. It has to be worked between the hands in order to soften it to a malleable state and is ready to use when it can be easily squeezed between thumb and forefinger.

Like fondant, ready-to-roll icing is easy to colour and flavour. It can be reworked as many times as you like because, unlike dough, it does not 'tighten' with use. The only limiting factor to the number of times you rework the icing is the amount of cake crumbs that you pick up in it. Best of all, it can be easily stored by wrapping tightly in a plastic freezer bag or something similar.

TEA This was an important part of the tea shop and a compromise over quality was never an option. The tea was always loose-leafed and a teabag was never seen in the shop. God forbid – my Grandmother would turn in her grave at the very thought of it.

Twinings Ceylon tea was used and it came in ten-pound bags, which were emptied on a daily basis. Of course, there was always traditional Earl Grey tea available, along with Darjeeling, Assam, Jasmine and, in the latter years, some popular herbal teas such as peppermint.

Coffee was also available. Not the lattes and mochaccinos you see in coffee houses today, but rather a strong traditional filter coffee using Lyons own brand, always served with hot milk and poured individually into the customer's cup from a pair of silver-plated coffee and milk pourers.

The pourers were made by Mappin & Webb of London. My father inherited them when his parents' tea shop in Westcliff closed. They were a matching set and could hold about a pint of liquid each. They were held by the waitresses by handles that were at right angles to the pouring spout so that their contents were poured by a twisting action of the wrists. There was a definite art in pouring from these containers. Many a new waitress, myself included, suffered the embarrassment of an overpour, by placing the spouts almost directly over the cups. It was never going to work like that.

When the shop closed, Peter had these 'pourers' re-plated so that they now look as good as new. They currently have pride of place in a display cabinet in my mother's dining room. They sit beside an engraved porcelain milk jug and plate from my great-grandparents' tea shop, *Beti's*. The porcelain not only has the name of the shop but also bears the Swiss flag, reflecting our ancestry in Poschiavo.

general baking tips

I have given specific tips for each recipe, but here are some more general baking tips to bear in mind.

CAKE TINS Use the size of cake tin recommended in each recipe.

Grease your tin with vegetable oil spray or butter and line it with baking parchment all around the inside – the base and sides.

For cakes requiring a long baking time (such as fruit cakes), Dad wrapped the exterior of tins with newspaper to ensure an even bake and to prevent scorching.

CREAMING Add eggs to a creamed mixture slowly, beating the mixture after each addition. If the mixture starts to curdle, beat in about 1 tablespoon of flour after each egg.

FOLDING I prefer to use a spatula when folding ingredients together. The traditional method is with a metal spoon, which is how Peter did it.

HOW TO KNOW WHEN A CAKE IS COOKED You can tell if a cake is ready in the following ways: sight, scent and touch. I have given all these indications where possible. I tend to insert a skewer, wait three seconds, then check it comes out clean and dry. If not, return the cake to the oven and try again after a few minutes. Light-textured cakes tend to shrink slightly away from the sides of the tins. You can also check if the cake is springy to the touch.

THE OVEN Ovens vary, even those of the same make, so cooking times may differ. The times given are a guide. Dad called his oven his 'faithful friend' so I recommend you get to know your oven.

Always preheat the oven prior to weighing ingredients. It must be at the correct temperature when the cake is ready to go in for best results.

The temperatures in this book refer to conventional ovens. Reduce the temperature by 20ºC for a fan oven.

I recommend the use of an oven thermometer for accuracy.

Bake cakes on the middle shelf of the oven. Unless specified, the centre of the oven is the best position for most cakes to ensure a good, even bake. I recommend meringues are placed near the bottom of the oven.

Try not to open the oven door during the first half of the baking time to prevent heat from escaping.

Meringues are a different case. Dad left his meringues on the lower shelf in the oven overnight, switched off, with the door ajar.

PASTRY-MAKING TIPS Below are Peter's suggestions, notes and rules-of-thumb on the art of pastry-making:

1 Ensure your hands and all your ingredients are cold. Cut the butter into cubes.
2 Make pastry by hand in a mixing bowl, directly on a work surface or in a food processor. Do not knead more than is necessary or whizz for too long in the food processor as your dough may toughen.
3 If the dough is sticky, add a sprinkling of flour.
4 Always rest the dough wrapped in cling film in the refrigerator for about 30 minutes to allow the gluten to relax.
5 When you remove the dough from the refrigerator, wait for a few minutes to allow it to come up to room temperature. If you attempt to roll it directly from the refrigerator it will constrict and may crumble.
6 The texture of your pastry will differ according to the flour and fat you use, plus the temperature and humidity.
7 If you make a base, prick the dough to allow air to penetrate and to prevent air bubbles forming (particularly with puff pastry).

8 You can brush pastry with egg wash (yolk and white) to give it a golden hue.

9 To bake blind, preheat oven to 200°C/gas mark 6. Line the flan tin with the pastry. Cover with baking parchment and fill with ceramic baking beans or dried pasta. Bake for 10–15 minutes until the pastry is partially cooked. Remove the parchment and beans or pasta. After baking blind, brush the pastry with a little egg wash. Return to the oven for a further 5 minutes. Remove from the oven, add your filling and continue to bake until both pastry and filling are cooked.

PREPARING EQUIPMENT FOR MAKING MERINGUES

When preparing to make meringues, clean your equipment thoroughly by pouring boiling water into the bowl of the freestanding mixer and over the beaters or the whisks on an electric hand-held whisk. Ensure they are dry before use.

SIFTING
Sift flour and any raising agents together for an even distribution of the raising agent throughout the flour. Sift icing sugar and cocoa, if using them, to eliminate any lumps they may contain.

WEIGHING
Dad used old-fashioned weights and instinct but he baked for over forty years! I use digital scales, on which you can put your bowl, set the scales to zero, add an ingredient, set the scales to zero again and carry on. This method of weighing is precise and saves on washing up.

YEAST
Dad used fresh yeast so I would recommend this but, like many people, I often use dried yeast, which is more readily available. In the recipes in this book, I provide instructions for using either dried or fresh yeast.

Finally, I recommend following not just the recipe but also your instinct, using all your senses to guide you as you bake. Keep notes to remind you of your decisions and discoveries. I now keep my laptop in the kitchen and note down changes to quantities, baking times, temperatures and so on.

CONVERSION TABLES
The recipes in this book use metric measurements but if, like my father, you prefer to work in Imperial, approximate conversions are below. Use either all metric or all Imperial measures, never a mixture of both.

weights

Metric	Imperial
8g	¼oz
15g	½oz
30g	1oz
60g	2oz
90g	3oz
120g	4oz
140g	5oz
175g	6oz
200g	7oz
225g	8oz
250g	9oz
285g	10oz
450g	16oz (1lb)
675g	1½lb
900g	2lb
1kg	2¼lb
1.5kg	3½lb
2kg	4½lb
2.3kg	5lb

volume

Metric	Imperial
5ml	1 teaspoon
10ml	2 teaspoons
20ml	1 tablespoon
25ml	1½ tablespoons (1 fl oz)
55ml	2 fl oz
75ml	3 fl oz
150ml	5 fl oz (¼ pint)
275ml	10 fl oz (½ pint)
570ml	1 pint
725ml	1¼ pint
1 litre	1¾ pint
1.2 litre	2 pints
1.5 litre	2½ pints
2.25 litres	4 pints

index

(t) denotes information in *baker's tips*
For birthday or other occasion cakes see *celebration cakes*
Eggs and similar store cupboard ingredients are indexed only when a main ingredient

almonds
  almond macaroons 177
  almond paste 96
  almond petit fours 125
  Bakewell tart 94
  Battenberg 64
  chocolate Florentines 54
  Christmas cake 76
  coffee Japonaise 174
  frangipane tart 51
  marzipan fruits 126
  mini macarons 178
  simnel cake 96
animal biscuits 26
apples
  apple cake 158
  apple dumplings 136
  Frankie's hot chutney 123
  traditional apple
    pie 137

bacon: Welsh rarebit 144 (t)
Bakewell tart 94
bananas: chocolate banana
  loaf 156
Battenberg 64
Belgian buns 168
biscuits 54
  animal biscuits 26
  biscuit bases (for
  cheesecakes) 50
  chocolate Florentines 54
  chocolate Viennese
    fingers 173
  Christmas biscuits 78
  coffee Japonaise 174
  heart-shaped biscuits 120
  Linzer biscuits 176
  shortbread 162
  traffic light biscuits 28
  Viennese whirls 172
Black Forest gateau 93
brandy: farmhouse
  fruitcake 107
bread 128–31
  white square sandwich
    loaf 140

buns
  Belgian buns 168
  chocolate éclairs 139 (t)
  choux buns 138
  hot cross buns 159
  Swiss buns 33
butter icing 172, 178
buttercream 34, 57–8,
  66, 71
  chocolate 173
  coffee 153, 169 (t), 174

cake tins 188
cakes (*large*)
  apple cake 158
  Battenberg 64
  Black Forest gateau 93
  caraway seed cake 70
  carrot cake 152
  cherry cake 48
  chocolate banana loaf 156
  chocolate-topped fresh
    cream sponge 156
  Christmas cake 76
  coffee and walnut
    cake 153
  Dundee cake 68
  farmhouse fruitcake 107
  Frankie's lemon drizzle
    cake 143
  ginger and date cake 158
  iced walnut cake 71
  lemon millefeuille 84–6
  Madeira sponge 67
  pink cottage cake 34–9
  simnel cake 96
  Swiss roll 169
  Victoria sponge 66
cakes (*small*)
  almond macaroons 177
  chocolate cornflake
    cakes 32
  chocolate cream slices 91
  coconut macaroons 90
  cream meringues 72
  Eccles cake 46
  English madeleines 59
  flapjacks 102

fondant fancies 57–8
fruit scones 46
palmiers 88
rock cakes 106
sponge fingers 24
Swiss cream pastry
  horns 170
teacakes 95
cakes, testing for
  'doneness' 188
caraway seed cake 70
carrot cake 152
celebration cakes
  Christmas cake 76
  pink cottage cake 34–9
  simnel cake 96
cheese
  cheese omelette 142
  quiche 143
  Welsh rarebit 144
cheesecake, lemon 50
cherries
  Black Forest gateau 93
  cherry cake 48
  chocolate Florentines 54
  Dundee cake 68
  English madeleines 59
  simnel cake 96
chillies: Frankie's hot
  chutney 123
chocolate 186
  animal biscuits 26
  Black Forest gateau 93
  buttercream 173
  chocolate banana loaf 157
  chocolate cream slices 91
  chocolate crunch 30
  chocolate éclairs 138
  chocolate fish 116–17
  chocolate Florentines 54
  chocolate peppermint
    creams 118
  chocolate Viennese
    fingers 173
  chocolate-topped fresh
    cream sponge 156
  choux buns 138
  coconut macaroons 90

coffee Japonaise 174
cream meringues 72 (t)
fondant fancies 57–8
heart-shaped biscuits 120
lemon millefeuille 84–6
rum truffles 102
Victoria sponge 66
choux buns 138
Christmas biscuits 78
Christmas cake 76
chutney
  Frankie's hot chutney 123
  tomato chutney 123
cocoa see chocolate
coconut, desiccated
  English madeleines 59
  macaroons 90
coffee
  coffee and walnut
    cake 153
  coffee buttercream 153,
    169 (t), 174
  coffee icing 139 (t)
  Swiss roll 169 (t)
confectionery and gifts
  almond petit fours 125
  chocolate fish 116–17
  chocolate Florentines 54
  chocolate peppermint
    creams 118
  Frankie's fudge 114
  marzipan fruits 126
  rum truffles 102
cornflakes: chocolate
  crunch 32
cream 184–5
  cream finger
    doughnuts 41
  cream horns 170
  cream meringues 72
  cream slices,
    chocolate 91
cream cheese
  lemon cheesecake 50
  topping 152 (t)
creaming 188
currants see dried fruits
custard tarts 134

damson jam 121
dates: ginger and date
  cake 160
decorating a cake 36–8
decorating biscuits 120 (t)
dips 57
doughnuts
  cream finger
    doughnuts 41
  jam doughnuts 40
dried fruits
  apple dumplings 136
  Christmas cake 76
  Dundee cake 68
  Eccles cake 46
  farmhouse fruitcake 107
  Frankie's hot chutney 123
  fruit scones 47
  hot cross buns 159
  mincemeat 77
  teacakes 95
dumplings, apple 136
Dundee cake 68

Eccles cake 46
éclairs, chocolate 139
eggs 184
  cheese omelette 142
  quiche 143
  Welsh rarebit 144
English madeleines 59

fairy cakes 25
fancies, fondant 57
farmhouse fruitcake 107
fats 184
flapjacks, Frankie's 102
Florentines, chocolate 54
flour 185
folding technique 188
fondant icing 118
  fondant fancies 57–8
  iced walnut cake 71
frangipane tart 51
Frankie's flapjacks 102
Frankie's fudge 114
Frankie's hot chutney 123
Frankie's lemon drizzle
  cake 150
fruit scones 47
fruitcake 107
fudge, Frankie's 114

gifts, edible see
  confectionery
ginger
  Frankie's hot chutney 123

ginger and date cake 160
  icing 158 (t)
glacé icing 25
glaze, spiced 159

ham
  quiche 143 (t)
  Welsh rarebit 144 (t)
heart-shaped biscuits 120
hot cross buns 159

icing 33, 51, 96, 168, 186–7
  butter icing 172, 178
  buttercream see
    buttercream
  coffee icing 139 (t)
  decorating biscuits 79
  fondant 57–8, 118
  ginger 158 (t)
  glacé 25

jam 185–6
  Bakewell tart 94
  damson jam 121
  jam doughnuts 40
  jam Swiss roll 169
  jam tarts 29
  jam truffles 102 (t)
  Linzer biscuits 176
  traffic light biscuits 28
  Victoria plum jam 121
Japonaise 174

lemon
  Frankie's lemon drizzle
    cake 143
  lemon cheesecake 50
  lemon curd 84
  lemon curd tarts 29 (t)
  lemon meringue pie 87
  lemon millefeuille 84–6
  Viennese whirls 172 (t)
Linzer biscuits 176

macarons:
  mini macarons 178
macaroons
  almond macaroons 177
  coconut macaroons 90
Madeira sponge 67
marmalade, Seville
  orange 122
marzipan fruits 126
meringues
  cream meringues 72
  lemon meringue pie 87
  tips on making 189
milk 184

mince pies 77
mincemeat 77
moulds
  for chocolate 116
  silicone 118
mushrooms: quiche 143 (t)

nuts
  flapjacks 102 (t)
  fudge 114
  see also walnuts

omelette, cheese 142
ovens 188

palmiers 88
pancakes, Scotch 41
pastry
  puff pastry 132
  shortcrust pastry 143
  sweet pastry 51, 52, 77,
    87, 133, 134
  tips on making 188–9
peppermint creams,
  chocolate 118
petit fours
  almond petit fours 125
  chocolate Florentines 54
pies
  mince pies 77
  traditional apple
    pie 137
pink cottage cake 34–9
plums: Victoria plum
  jam 121
porridge oats: flapjacks 102
puff pastry 132

quiche 143

Rice Krispies: chocolate
  crunch 32 (t)
rock cakes 106
rolling pins 26 (t)
rose water: almond
  petit fours 125
rum truffles 102

scones, fruit 47
Scotch pancakes 41
Seville orange
  marmalade 122
shortbread 162
shortcrust pastry 143
  sweet 51, 52, 77, 87,
    133, 134
sifting 189
simnel cake 96

sponge
  Black Forest gateau 93
  chocolate-topped fresh
    cream sponge 156
  English madeleines 59
  fondant fancies 57–8
  Madeira sponge 67
  sponge fingers 24
  vanilla sponge 34
  Victoria sponge 66
strawberry tarts 52
sugar syrup glaze 185
sultanas see dried fruits
sweet shortcrust pastry
  133, 134
sweets see confectionery
  and gifts
Swiss buns 33
Swiss cream pastry
  horns 170
Swiss roll 169

tarts (savoury): quiche 143
tarts (sweet)
  Bakewell tart 94
  custard tarts 134
  frangipane tart 51
  jam tarts 29
  lemon meringue pie 87
  strawberry tarts 52
  treacle tart 108
teacakes 95, 187
tomato chutney 123
traffic light biscuits 28
treacle tart 108
truffles, rum 102

vanilla sponge 34
Victoria plum jam 121
Victoria sponge 66
Viennese fingers,
  chocolate 173
Viennese whirls 172

walnuts
  coffee and walnut
    cake 153
  iced walnut cake 71
weighing ingredients 189
Welsh rarebit 144

yeast 189

acknowledgements

I would like to thank everyone who has helped me during the creation of *The Baker's Daughter*.

My brilliant agent, Caroline Michel, and Anna Jean-Hughes, her assistant.

Mum, who shared stories and photographs from the tea shop, helped during the baking classes with Dad, baked all the tea shop classics and re-tested recipes.

My siblings, who all shared memories of our childhood through stories, baking and photographs. Johnny was tireless in his attention to detail, ensuring Dad's baking legacy lives on. Fuby, the baker's youngest daughter, could be relied on for conversations about cakes and turning up with plates of animal biscuits, cream horns and madeleines. Gordon shared stories, photos and his versions of Dad's recipes.

My nephews, Chris and Nick, and my niece, Hannah: thank you for all the photographs with Dad's cakes.

Aunty Mary and Aunty Hazell, thank you for telling me all about growing up with Dad in your family tea shop, *Lane's*, in Westcliff.

The Forer family: Bernadette Forer's history of our family was invaluable in helping me to trace my pastry chef ancestors to Poschiavo, and her photographs, including those of the café in Poschiavo, are family treasures; Angela Forer, who provided stories and photographs from *Beti's* tea shop in Ryde.

Diana Wood from the Historic Ryde Society for supplying photographs and information.

Mandy Marodeen, thank you for your photograph of Peter's grandchildren.

Edward Taylor, for the illustration of *Peter's* that decorates the inside cover of the book.

William Sitwell, Editor of *Waitrose Kitchen*, who commissioned me to write an article about being a baker's daughter, with some recipes from the tea shop.

Liz Gough, former Editorial Director at Pan Macmillan, who spotted the article and introduced me to such a wonderful publishing house.

The Pan Macmillan team: Jon Butler, Non-Fiction Publisher, for his passion for this book; Cindy Chan, Commissioning Editor, who was a delight to work with throughout the fascinating editing process. Thanks also to Jennifer Kerslake, Editorial Assistant, Tania Wilde, Head of Editorial Services, Laura Carr, Desk Editor, Jonathan Pelham, Jacket Designer and Ben Chisnall, Production Controller.

Simon Daley, art director and designer: thank you, Simon, for conveying my family's old-fashioned tea shop and traditional cakes to a modern audience, creatively mixing old and new.

Salima Hirani, copyeditor, for editing the text and making us feel at home at the shoot. Also Rachel Malig for her meticulous proofread.

The shoot team: photographer Ian Garlick, food stylist Kathryn Hawkins, and hair and make-up artist Debbie Parr.

Recipe testers: as well as my family, I had reliable and resourceful testers: Samuel Goldsmith, who helped at a key early stage, Joyce Bendall, who worked with Dad in the bakehouse and knows the recipes so well; Polly McCowen, and Miranda Keyes.

Friends: Karen Ascough, who shared stories from the tea shop and joined in with Dad's baking masterclasses (we had a lot of fun!); Alice Driscoll, for all the childhood cake stories and support.

Amanda Ribbans, who designed my website and created my original family tea shop tree; and Lulu O'Hagan.

My writing circle: Al, Lisa and Janette.

Writers: Dr M. G. Stephens, who motivated me to write about the tea shop in a writer's workshop. Dr Tracy Brain and Dr Mimi Thebo from Bath Spa University, for challenging me on my writing and baking journey, and thanks to Tracy for providing a photograph of the chocolate fish. Orlando Murrin, food writer and inspiration. Shaun Phillips, Tony Turnbull, Suzy Greaves, Tamasin Day-Lewis and Rachel Stammers.

The Roux family: Albert Roux, for reading early drafts, encouraging me and providing the Foreword. Cheryl Roux, for her help and kindness, and Michel Roux Jr.

Former customers and staff: all those who shared memories of *Peter's*.

My children: thank you Lara and Joe for baking with me and for being so good while I wrote our family story. You are the next generation of bakers.